POWER OF SAMSON: GUARDIAN OF GOD'S SECRET CODE

D.H. ALEXANDER

Cover art by Jose Razo.
Illustrations by Loren Rodriguez.

The Front Cover: What do the Jawbone and the Locks represent? How could Samson be one of the elect **Great Cloud of Witnesses** in the Bible? *And what shall I more say? for the time would fail me to tell of Gedeon, and [of] Barak, and [of]* **Samson**... *Who through faith subdued kingdoms, wrought righteousness, obtained promises,* **stopped the mouths of lions**... *Wherefore seeing we also are compassed about with so great a cloud of witnesses, let us lay aside every weight, and the sin which doth so easily beset [us], and let us run with patience the race that is set before us...* **Hebrews 11:32, 33; 12:1** *And what does the Gate symbolize? the gates of hell shall not prevail* **Matthew 16:18**

Accounts based upon actual events.

ISBN: 978-1-952229-03-09

Sword Bearers Ministries
PO Box 2010 Richland, Washington

Preface and Dedication

You and I are among the most majestic of creatures ever to have graced the surface of the planet home we call Earth. We dream, we dance, we create, we live, and we have dominion over all other animals. We send humans to the moon, probe the outer limits of our solar system, view the ends of the universe from orbiting telescopes and satellites, build skyscrapers, harness the atom, and regrettably build weapons of mass destruction. Yet with all of our genius, science gives us no way of escape from eternal slumber. Our probes from space show our planet as nothing more than an infinitesimally small speck in the fringes of the Milky Way galaxy. Our smallness seems to render our existence inconsequential. We've watched as those around us succumb to the pains of aging, cancer, heart disease, suicide, murder, and accidental death. Consequently, few scientists believe in God nor the promise of an eternal life. They see it as a cruel figment of our imagination and a placebo for the masses. I was skeptical of the existence of God.

But an incredible discovery revealed in this book provides reproducible, objective evidence that God Exists. As this Book attests, my beloved wife spent many a restless night pointing and guiding me in the Way of Truth. Without her encouragement, this book would never have been written and I would have missed out on eternal life. This book is dedicated to my wife, my mom and dad, my siblings, my family, my son, my six daughters, my grandchildren, my friends and co-workers, the scientific community, unbelievers, doubters, my church family, my bible students, and editors that they may have the confidence and comfort that the God of Israel is real.

This book is for you and those that you care about.

D.H.ALEXANDER

Table of Contents

He that sits above the wheels of the heavenly chariot still guides the affairs of mankind[1]

In the context of the vastness of space and the immensity of time we are as nothing. Why would anyone care?

Soon there will be Time no Longer![2]
Is God in control of your destiny?

---

1 Ezekiel 10:1-4; Ezekiel 1:4-28.
2 Revelation 10:6.

PROLOGUE:
SCIENCE or GOD?

It all started in September of 1996. In the early days of our courtship, my wife took me to a seminar in Washington State. One of my business associates that I knew from Washington D.C. inexplicably welcomed us at the door and directed us to our seats. What was he doing here? Steve's presence seemed strangely out of place. I wondered how the two of us ended up together in this seminar 3000 miles from where we had worked as co-workers. If he hadn't been there to greet us, I probably wouldn't have taken the time to listen to what the evangelist had to say. As soon as I glanced at the big screen in the auditorium, I wanted to turn right around and walk out. For on that screen was a picture of a supernatural beast ridden by a woman, called "Babylon the Great" drinking a goblet of wine that looked like blood.[3]

Years later, Steve told me that I was the last one he'd ever expected to walk through that door. He'll confirm that today if you ask him. After all, I had a reputation of being a skeptic in the realm of science and I had a predisposition to worldliness and its snares of sin. The speaker was Russell C. Burrill, an evangelist who provided prophetic interpretations of the seemingly impenetrable Books of Daniel and Revelation. The moment I saw the beasts of Revelation, I was convinced that the woman that brought me to the meeting unknowingly belonged to a cult. I thought that she and others in the audience were being brain-washed and taken advantage of. I spent more time surveying the people in the audience than listening to the speaker. But on the other end of the spectrum, Steve believed somehow in all this strange imagery. And just recently Steve's wife Dee tells me that Steve was surprised yet excited when he saw me walk into the auditorium because he was convinced that God was going to do something special with my life.

---

3 Revelation 17:5.

At the time, I firmly believed that we should live each day as if it were our last because I was sure that the grave offered nothing but dust. Many of my colleagues in science have wrestled with the existence of God. I wasn't about to accept something I couldn't see or examine; nor should you. I would accept nothing less than solid verifiable facts! Give me ***objective evidence;* no *leap of faith*** for me…and no hideous beasts! To me Science was supreme.

Can you imagine the magnitude of a Biblical Flood that would cover all of the world's mountain tops? After all, if the Genesis Flood waters truly covered the mountain tops in the account of Noah, then where did all the water go? More than that, why did the beasts mysteriously come to Noah's Ark two by two as if called by some unseen Being? Sounds like folklore. What else could it be? Later my wife went to her library and had me watch films on the subject, even a film narrated by a well-known radionuclide scientist in my field of geochemistry by the name of Robert Gentry from Oak Ridge National Laboratory. I had read his works on Polonium radiohalos so I wondered how someone of his stature could possibly believe in God. I was determined to rescue my wife from the grip that the Church seemed to have on her. But her staunch refusal to change her beliefs drove me even more intensely to disprove her Scriptures. And thankfully she didn't budge an inch due to my scientific "reasoning."

As a practicing geochemist I was trained to believe in the gradual evolution of our universe, our planet, and life. Scientists in my field are trained that the Earth is billions of years old. We accept these principles as guiding truths and as the anchors of our research. So how can we, how could I, accept the Bible as the Word of God? The supernatural world of the Tanakh, the Bible, and the Qur'an are in stark contrast to the natural world of science. The realms of the natural and supernatural are like two independent and seemingly incompatible universes. Scientists often assume that an invisible supernatural universe is a figment of the imagination. They see "God" as a placebo for the masses to comfort their acceptance of death. But what if a supernatural universe does exist? What if miracles and visions of angels really do occur? Scientists continue to seek the "God particle" and investigate black holes, dark matter, dark energy, gravity waves, and other unseen phenomena. I was sure that if God existed, His intelligence would be reflected in the writings of the Bible. And as it turns out, that is precisely the case that I'll soon show you. *If God exists He would have great powers and unbounded intelligence; His Bible must have great depth of meaning and provide prophecies of the future that would set it upon a pinnacle, far above any of the great pieces of literature ever written.* Simply put, if its assertions are true, then the Bible would be the "***Book of Books***." Does the Bible bear the fingerprint of God or not? What would God's "fingerprint" look like? Why not investigate the supernatural Bible with scientific methods that we apply to these other unseen phenomena? Could an unseen supernatural universe actually exist? Hypothetically, consider for a moment the power and intelligence of a God that could create the world by merely speaking it into existence as the Scriptures claim! Such a God would have an immeasurable and infinite IQ and unimaginable POWER. Could His Word be the cause of the Big Bang? If God is truly omniscient, then He can see the events of the future as clearly as He can see events of the past. No mortal has these powers. After all, scientists have great difficulty predicting tomorrow's weather, let alone far distant future events.

Smoking Gun

Until the year 2000, I was viewing the events of the Bible through the theories of science. I soon became even more dissuaded that God exists. By the year 2000, I had had enough of the discussion of religion. I decided, then and there, to use scientific methods to prove to my wife that the Scriptures were simply the wishful fables and legends of men. So I stepped out on a journey to disprove the Bible, leaving open the remote possibility that the Bible could be true. Out of my ignorance, I decided to challenge God. One fateful evening in January of 2000, as I sat in my office reading the account of Joseph in the last fourteen chapters of the Book of Genesis, I prayed to God and challenged Him to prove to me that He was behind the writings of the Scriptures, that is, if He existed or cared.

Within minutes, I sat shaken by an Emmaus experience as I gazed upon the evidence in my hands like a smoking gun. It was as if God dropped scales from my eyes. Looking back I realize now that God had given me a lesson in the power of prayer. And one thing I've learned is that God answers prayers. As I looked upon the Scriptures, I could scarcely believe what He unlocked for me…and for you. Because what I beheld was ***infallible proof*** of the existence of God. And for whatever His purpose, God chose to answer my prayer and put me to work for Him. What I saw was the testable, reproducible kind of evidence that scientists had been seeking through the ages. I was stunned by what I saw. But what was I to do? I couldn't see any other logical explanation. It clearly proved the existence of God. But shortly after my experience I rationalized that I myself had imagined the experience. I soon transitioned to a state of denial. After all, how could it be true? But a nagging voice kept pushing me to continue digging into the concealed message that had been revealed. Was the hidden message isolated to the account of Joseph or could it be found elsewhere?

A monumental study was in order. Emotion had to be set aside. The evidence must provide the verdict. Science has taught me to be skeptical and objective. Besides, in scientific circles, the discussion of religion is virtually taboo. For more than two decades I conducted systematic scientific studies of the Old Testament and today I stand armed with overwhelming evidence to make the case for God. Instead of disproving God, God soon proved to me that He's alive. By the year 2000 my world view shifted from science to God. Why believe in God? Why believe in the Bible? Why believe in the realm of the Supernatural and life after death? Today I realize that there's more at stake than your physical life. Your eternal life is at stake too!

1 *Does God Exist?*

"All scripture is given by inspiration of God, and is profitable for doctrine, for reproof, for correction, for instruction in righteousness: that the man of God may be perfect, thoroughly furnished unto all good works."[4]

I gathered the precious scrolls under my arm and headed into the ivy covered building on the center of the campus. After less than a year I'd found mysterious[5] patterns throughout the Old Testament Scriptures. I systematically recorded the patterns on scrolls that surely could be explained by theologians. The local pastors were unable to give me a satisfactory explanation so I sought the answer in academia. I'd been sharing my discoveries with a very close friend of mine; a nuclear chemist by the name of Dr. Nabil Marcos. Nabil and I had collaborated on several patents and we had developed a very close relationship. We think of each other as brothers. Nabil was a skeptic like myself; a *doubting Thomas* you might say. Yet the more I explained my findings to Nabil, the more we realized that I'd found something profound. But it was beyond our understanding. It turned out that Nabil had colleagues in a nearby theology department and made arrangements for my visit. As I ascended the stairs of the old ivy covered university building I felt a rush of excitement. I had the feeling that at long last I'd get an explanation of my mysterious findings. After several meetings in the Theology Department I was finally directed to Dr. Peter Stevanoff.[6] Peter's a prominent theologian renowned for his expertise in unlocking prophecy. As I made my way to his office I wondered how he'd receive my analyses.

---

4 2 Timothy 3:16, 17.
5 Mark 4:11.
6 Name changed for anonymity.

When I entered his office I was greeted by a large man, well over six feet with a large smile on his face that was genuine. "Good morning professor, I'm Dr. Alexander." This gentle giant of a man warmly extended his large hand and I immediately knew somehow that this was the man that would have the answers I needed. "Good morning Dr. Alexander, I've been expecting you. Please call me Peter," he said with a distinct Eastern European accent. "And please call me Don." I immediately felt relaxed as if I was meeting with a long lost friend. As I struggled with the large set of scrolls he pointed to a table where I could unroll them and he asked, "What do you have here Don?"

"Peter, before I show you the scrolls I first need an answer. Do you really, I mean really believe in God?" Taken somewhat aback he said, "Of course I do. What are you driving at Don?" "Simple really. Can you point me to physical evidence of the existence of God?" "Why do you ask?" "The scientists and atheists that I want to witness to need something besides faith. Is there anything that theologians can offer scientists besides philosophical arguments?" "Not really. There's the intelligent design findings that we call the teleological argument. But I'm sure you know more about that than I do." "I'm very aware of the argument Peter. But as powerful as it is, scientists still scoff at the idea." "Then there's the cosmological argument." "Not sure I understand the significance of that argument." "At some point in time nothing existed, yet the Being we call God brought everything into existence. How could it have taken place without God?" "Makes some sense but again, that's philosophical. Some scientists are claiming it all started from nothing. We need evidence if we're to convince the scientific community. The big question is whether or not theologians have proof of the existence of God?" "Don, I've studied prophecy and it provides me the faith I need. How else can you explain the exact fulfillment of the time prophecies of Daniel and Revelation?" "I agree that the prophecies are amazing Peter. But I'm not looking for a faith argument. I need facts." "I'm sorry Don. Of course we have archaeological information that authenticates actual historical Biblical events. But if I understand you correctly, I don't think we have the kind of evidence that you're looking for. Besides prophecy, we have miracles but I don't suppose that would answer their skepticism. If that's not sufficient then I'm not sure I can offer you anything. I wish I had the physical evidence you're looking for but I don't."

"Well, if I'm correct Peter, my findings are of a special form of prophecy. I believe that they provide the proof that we've both been looking for." I pointed to the table covered with the scrolls. "I've been recording mysterious patterns from the Scriptures. I've been finding them throughout the Old Testament and I hoped that you might be able to explain what I've been finding." As we opened them one by one a wide smile came over his face. I knew I'd come to the right place.

Great Cloud of Witnesses

Wherefore seeing we also are compassed about with so GREAT A CLOUD OF WITNESSES, let us lay aside every weight, and the sin which doth so easily beset [us], and let us run with patience the race that is set before us[7]

"Don, before we begin evaluating your scrolls, could you please tell me a little about your background and what led you to this meeting. Based upon a quick glance at your scrolls, I'm convinced that your visit here is not by accident. You've come by a divine appointment." Strangely I had wondered myself if our meeting was guided by an unseen hand.

"Well. I'm a nuclear chemist, having spent much of my career traveling around the world evaluating technologies that can be used to process nuclear waste. Scientists in my community believe in an old Earth. They mock the basic statements of the Bible, especially accounts of the Creation and the Flood. Frankly, they can't see how the Bible and our current state of science can be reconciled. So they scoff at the Scriptures. For many years I had given up my faith too. I couldn't reconcile science with the

---

7 Hebrews 12:1

Scriptures, especially as recorded in the Book of Genesis." After about a half hour of trading information about my past we started to focus on the real issues.

"Now, tell me again why you're here." I felt like I was being Cross-examined at a confessional. "Well, at a dark moment in my life, I set forth to disprove that the writings of the Old Testament Scriptures were written by God through the Holy Spirit as they claim: *All scripture [is] given by inspiration of God.*[8]" "Why?"

"Frankly my wife believes that the Scriptures are Truth. But my background and training convinced me otherwise." He nodded and I continued as if he'd heard this story before. "Well, since Darwin's *"Origin of the Species"* and Lyell's theory of *"uniformitarianism"* there's been a rapid falling away from a belief in God within my field and the scientific community. Even my childhood churches are emptying as if they've given up their faith in the existence of God. Long ago I came to the conclusion that the Scriptures are no more than a historical compilation of the works of men because they're inconsistent with science." "Then why all this study?" He waved his hand at the scrolls.

"I wanted to disprove the Scriptures because I didn't want to waste our weekends. But my wife was passionate about them. So I set out to search for flaws within the Bible so I could toss it out. I didn't want to waste my life wrapped up in the whole church thing. I was convinced she was wrong." An almost compassionate grin crossed his face as he gestured for me to continue. "Go on please."

"So I set forth to disprove the Bible but I was determined to remain objective and leave open the incredible possibility that the Scriptures are written through the inspiration of God's Spirit. If God is the author, there should be evidence of His fingerprint on the ancient scrolls. Right?" "Of course!" he nodded.

"So I was determined to use scientific methods of my profession to interrogate the Scriptures. I knew it would be an enormous task

---

8 2 Timothy 3:16.

but I was determined. But think about it Peter. What would it take to demonstrate the existence of God to the scientific community? Have you dealt with scientists struggling to get to the truth?"

"Of course but only with limited success. Though I must admit, I don't think I've ever met anyone so determined to prove the authenticity of the Scriptures using scientific methods. Why not prove the existence of God through the evidence seen in the physical world through your science?"

"Scientists are trained to believe that life has evolved over billions of years. Most believe that landforms gradually evolve. We accept these principles as guiding truths and as the foundation and paradigm of modern day earth science. So how could I, or any scientist for that matter, accept the Bible as the Word of God?"

"Don, what do you think it would take to convert scientists?" "Well, the evidence would have to be far more convincing than the archeological confirmations of the Bible. I can tell you that!" "And why not?" "Archaeology verifies the historical basis of the Bible, but it won't convince any self-respecting scientist that a supernatural world exists." "Then what do you think it'd take?"

"It would have to be far more convincing than the prophetic claims of ancient writers." He winced as I continued. "I'm not meaning to belittle your profession but it would have to be more convincing than Jesus' own claims that He was the Messiah and that after three days and three nights He would be resurrected.[9] For a scientist, the Scriptures would have to be the fulfillment of all of these lines of evidence and more if they're truly the inspiration of a Living God. We'd need to provide them with testable, measureable, reproducible evidence to make the case. If Jesus is the Messiah as He claims, all the prophecies, symbolic language, and parables would have to be fulfilled in Him and through His Plan to save mankind from Satan and his fallen angels. If Jesus isn't the Messiah, the evidence will show that the basis of the Bible is inconsistent, incongruent, and contradictory."

---

9 Matthew 12:40.

"That's a pretty tall order. People have been working on this for two thousand years. What would it take to get scientists to even take the time to look at such a proof if you came up with it? Or what makes you think that theologians like myself would toss out our beliefs because of any inconsistencies or incongruencies that you might come up with? Couldn't you make the case from the perspective of science?"

"Maybe Peter, but scientists that have tried to approach it from the physical world have failed. Recently, those that have professed intelligent design and have claimed that the universe is here by a Being known as God are being scoffed at." "I see your point."

"I was looking for hard facts not faith. I had to find evidence one way or another and convince myself first. At first I had serious reservations. I mean, how could all these lines of evidence align without contradiction? In fact I was convinced that the internal arguments in the Scriptures would be contradictory." "I'm sure you know that there are some inconsistencies even in the Gospels." "I'm not talking about differences in perspectives, timing, or grammar. I'm talking about irreconcilable contradictions."

"But with all your skepticism why'd you bother?" "Well, I soon realized that few scientists have ever read the Bible let alone interrogated its depths. Most discredit the Bible based upon beliefs rather than evidence based upon hard facts, just as many of the scribes and Pharisees had done at the time of Christ. If I were to dismiss the Bible, I knew I would be just like them. So I set forth in January of 2000 to conduct my own research. I'd have to make an ironclad case. What I discovered profoundly changed my life."

"Are you suggesting that you've found something that will make the case?" "Yes, I believe so. That's why I've come here today to discuss my discovery; confidentially of course."

Peter asked with his eastern European accent, "Confidential of course! What is it that you've found that's so convincing?" "I've found that the Old Testament is filled with a Great Cloud of Witnesses that guard the evidence that Jesus is the Messiah and that His Plan of Salvation is fast coming to an end." "Incredible! I haven't ever heard anyone put it that way before. Can you show me an example?" "Sure!" I pointed to the scrolls as I continued. "Have you considered the Bible superhero Samson?" "Samson? Sure I've read and studied his account in the Book of Judges. How does his account provide the kind of evidence you've been looking for?" "Within his account and so many other Old Testament superheroes, there's a hidden code that makes proof positive that God exists and His Plan is unfolding as we speak. Based on my studies I predict that we aren't far from the climax of the Plan and the end of time." "I've come to the same conclusion. Time is short." "So I set forth to examine the Bible itself to see if the Cross is truly at the heart of infinity."

"So what've you found that's so profound that you've changed your mind?" "Over the past several months, I've found that the hidden Code guarded by Samson and a Great Cloud of Witnesses provides far greater proof of the existence of God than the amazing set of balanced physical constants that hold our Universe together."

"Without a doubt, a growing number of scientists are making claims that the universe must have been created by an exceptionally intelligent Being or Beings. They're arriving at their conclusions based upon an examination of a large and growing number of physical constants ranging from nuclear forces, gravitational forces, electromagnetic forces, and the cosmological constant.[10]" "I've read about the teleological argument of the Grand Designer. I would agree that the magnitude of these physical constants appears to rule-out any reasonable possibility that our universe originated through a set of random events. If I understand these arguments, if any of the five universal constants were changed minutely, the universe and life as we know it could not exist." I nodded in agreement as he continued. "According to some physicists I've talked with, if we increase the strength of the gravitational constant by even an extremely small amount, the universe couldn't have life sustaining planets. If the gravitational

10 The Privileged Planet. G. Gonzalez and J. Richards. 444 pages. March, 2004. Regnery Publishing

force is too strong the stars will burn up too quickly and if it is too weak the planets and stars couldn't form. How can these constants be explained as a freak coincidence of nature?" I was amazed that a theologian had such an appreciation of the physical arguments.

"You're quite right Peter. The cosmological constant represents a balance between the attractive force of gravity which tends to cause the universe to collapse and the repulsive force speculated to be dark matter and dark energy that fill the voids of space. These attractive and repulsive forces are perfectly balanced within an exceedingly narrow margin. If it's slightly positive the universe would fly apart and if it's slightly negative it would collapse."

"Don, don't you think that these arguments, that you refer to as *fine tuning*, make a compelling case for the origination of a universe by a Creator God rather than by chance?" "I do. But the scientific literature's filled with skepticism. Recently, some of the world's greatest minds, like Dr. Lawrence Krauss and Dr. Richard Dawkins have made a mockery of God and Creation, claiming that the universe evolved from nothing."[11] "Well Don, nothing comes from nothing, nothing ever does."[12] "I agree with you Peter. These scientists invoke quantum mechanics, the Heisenberg uncertainty principle, and concepts like the quantum vacuum to make their case and defy the origin of the universe by a Creator. The works of Krauss and Dawson and many others are forcing a confrontation between science and religion. Fundamentally, did the universe come from an accidental Big Bang or from the Word of God?[13]" "Don, if God did speak the worlds[14] into existence, His Word would truly be omnipotent, do you agree?" "Peter, my thesis is that if God exists His fingerprint would be in the Scriptures." "I agree Don. Perhaps that's why His Word is so powerful? So what were you looking for?" "Well, I wanted to determine whether there's evidence that the Scriptures themselves, as they claim to be, are of a supernatural origin or not. So after

---

11 A Universe from Nothing: Why There Is Something Rather than Nothing. Lawrence M. Krauss, initially published on January 10, 2012 by Free Press.
12 Sound of Music. Richard Rogers and Oscar Hammerstein. November 1959.
13 Psalm 33:8 and 9.
14 Hebrews 1:2.

months of research, testable patterns have emerged that give evidence of the existence of God. I want you to explain them." "Tell me about them."

"Well imagine for a moment that we were to find encrypted events that predict the steps of Christ more than a thousand years in advance? What if we were to find these codes in dozens of places throughout the Old Testament as the fingerprint of God? What if a set of chosen Guardians held portions of the Code as a treasure map in the form of a multidimensional cryptogram? They do as you'll soon see!" "Fascinating! I came to the same fundamental conclusion years ago based on my studies of the Old Testament prophecies."

So I opened the scrolls and I showed Peter the hidden encrypted pattern of events in the life of Samson. The author of the Scriptures provided irrefutable evidence of the events in the life of Christ more than a thousand years in advance. The supernatural author conceals symbolic connections as algebraic expressions within literary images. The symbols are so clear and thought provoking that even those young children that study with me like Jamil, Elvin, Hasiel, Christopher, and Shannon understand their deeper meaning. Step by step, I discovered 52 parallel symbolic events hidden within the account of Samson that are connected to the account of Jesus from their births to their deaths. The probability of finding these 52 events in the same temporal order is like finding a single atom in an undisclosed location in the universe blind-folded. The results are frankly mind boggling.

"Well Don, your findings are convincing to me. But how do you think they'll be received by other scientists?" "Well there are many more witnesses like Samson and there's far more evidence that the Scriptures are inspired by God. There are continuous patterns that are woven throughout the Scriptures written over a period of more than a thousand years. I've traced these patterns from Genesis to Revelation. Who but the Holy Spirit could have guided the minds of men to record the Scriptures as a symphony?"

"I think I understand. Could you explain further?" "Peter, the events in the life of Jesus are deliberately embedded and intertwined in the account of Samson. At first I thought my findings were coincidence but I soon realized it was deliberate. I soon found that the account of Jesus is hidden in dozens of other Old Testament characters more than a thousand years in advance." "Dozens?" "Yes. I've brought others to show you." "So Don, what do you think it all means?" "Well, I can only conclude that the embedded code found in such a *Great Cloud of Witnesses* establishes an *infallible proof* [15] of the existence of God far more convincing than the *"fine tuning"* arguments coming from the realm of science. Taken together, the hidden code and the finely tuned physical constants provide the ultimate proof that God exists."

"I agree with you Don but don't forget the prophecies and the archaeological evidence. And I must admit, I've never seen it unfolded this way. It is a miraculous prophetic revelation that the events in the life of Christ are embedded in the life of Samson more than a thousand years in advance." "Well Peter, the importance of the work doesn't stop there. It's the beginning for you and me. It provides a single portion of a grand treasure map that when assembled with the portions of the Code held in secret by other "Guardians" like Samson, allows us to piece together the events that will usher in the soon return of Jesus Christ."

Samson's Golden Keys

Samson's Power isn't fully unleashed until you realize that the account applies to you. Like Samson, we all grow up and leave home, we confront Satan, we go through trials and temptations, and each of us are captives in this decrepit world with no way of escape but through death. Yet God has given you, like Samson, a purpose for your life. And He has given you the opportunity of an everlasting life. And He will fill you with the Holy Spirit to face the adversary, just as He did for Samson.

---

15 Acts 1:3

Samson's account reveals seven golden keys and much more in the form of fascinating riddles, revealing parables, and metaphors that connect Samson to Christ:

1. Riddle of the garments;
2. Riddle of the foxes sent to set the Philistine fields on fire;
3. Riddle of the jawbone;
4. Riddle of the city gate;
5. Riddle of Delilah;
6. Riddle of Samson's hair; and
7. Riddle of the House of Dagon.

Deciphering the meaning of these seven golden keys provides the evidence that God exists. Yet when we finish with our spiritual archaeological dig of Samson we'll have only uncovered the single wheel of Samson. There are enumerable wheels left to uncover. Just as an archaeologist that begins with the discovery of a single ancient clue like the writing on a single cornerstone. Just as that clue may be the key to a long lost civilization, we begin with Samson as our cornerstone that will unlock the door to eternity.

In this *"Guardians of God's Secret Code"* series we uncover wheel after wheel guarded by a *"Great Cloud of Witnesses"* which collectively expose more of the Grand Tapestry of the Bible. We'll see the great mystery of life and death, the world past, and the world to come and in so doing, we'll discover the Kingdom of God.

Samson is the Superman of the Old Testament Scriptures performing feats far beyond the limits of power ever performed by other men. Yet His power is but a shadow of the power of the WORD of God which *"is quick, and powerful, and sharper than any two-edged sword, piercing even to the dividing asunder of soul and spirit..."*[16]

---

16 Hebrews 4:12.

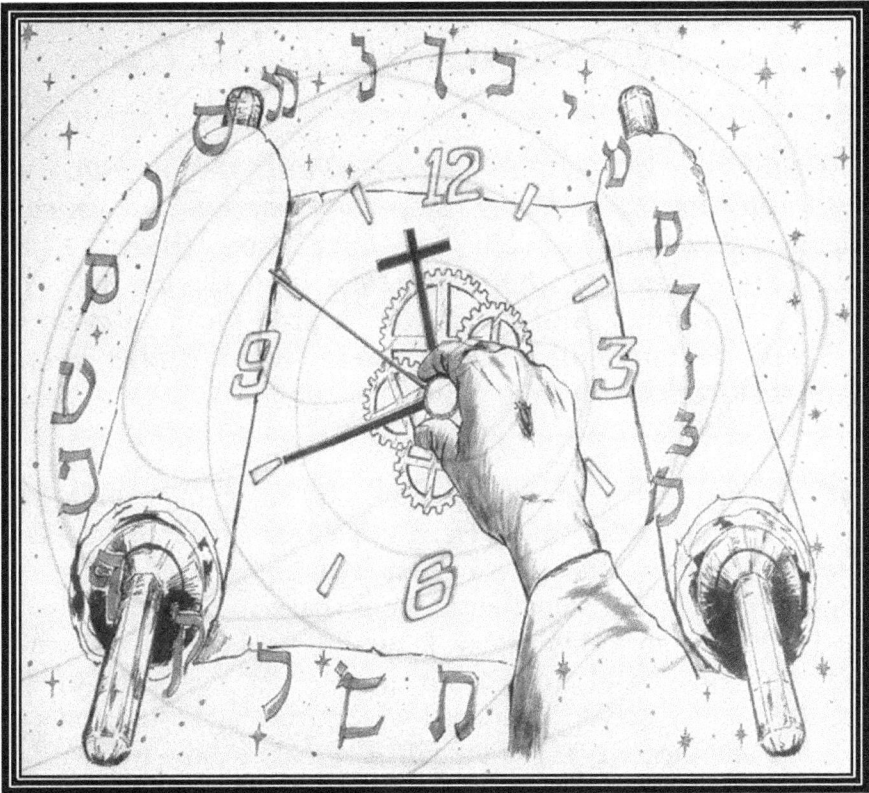

HAND UPON THE WHEEL: The Divine Hand is upon the intricate wheels of world history guiding the Plan of Salvation to completion. He that has the power over the rise and fall of kingdoms is steadily bringing human history to a close. The world's end time events are encrypted in the Holy Scriptures for seekers to find. Knock and it shall be opened unto you.[17]

---

17 Matthew 7:7.

2 Supernatural Birth

And the angel of the LORD appeared unto the woman, and said unto her, Behold now, thou [art] barren, and bearest not: but thou shalt conceive, and bear a son. [Judges 13:3] Then said Mary unto the angel, How shall this be, seeing I know not a man? And Mary said, Behold the handmaid of the Lord; be it unto me according to thy word. And the angel departed from her. [Luke 1:34, 38]

C hange was in the making or should I say in the remaking of an unbeliever. One evening in February of 1999, JaNa and I knelt by the side of our bed and prayed, with the conviction that God would answer our prayer. We pleaded with God to add another child to our family of six daughters. We had faith that God could work a miracle, even at this stage of my journey. So we prayed, sinful as I was, "Dear Father forgive us of our sins and please grant us the gift of a male child. We ask that he be healthy and grow to serve you."

Within two weeks we had taken the over-the-counter home test that proved positive for JaNa's pregnancy. We were certain that God had granted our request, just as we had asked. Soon we had the sonogram that proved that the child was a boy. We were more confident than ever that the child was the gift we requested from God.

But, a couple weeks later we met with the doctor. He solemnly went through the evidence and recommended an abortion. He said that for people of my age group a genetic defect in the fetus was very likely. ***"The chance is greater than 1 in 25 that the child will have a genetic defect, maybe 1 in 10."*** We wouldn't buy the doctor's prognosis. We remained convinced that the pregnancy was an answer to our prayer. He proposed many tests including amniocentesis but we only agreed to a blood test. We told the doctor to order the test and we went home and prayed. A couple weeks later the results of the test ruled out a genetic defect. Again we gave thanks to God.

Shortly after the birth of our healthy baby boy, members of our church asked if they could use him as baby Jesus in the Christmas play. Imagine the turn-around that this meant in our lives. We were blessed by the gift of a new creation in the form of our baby boy and in the re-Creation that was taking place in my heart and mind. And serendipitously, the role of our son as baby Jesus in the Christmas pageant drew my attention to the miracle births of Isaac, Jacob (and Esau), Joseph, Samson, Samuel, John, and Jesus. And Samson takes the central high position among the seven!

Shortly after our baby's birth, I started to seek evidence to make an "iron clad" case that God exists. Convincing me was one thing; convincing the scientific community is an entirely different matter. The more I interrogated the Scriptures, the more I became certain that God was the life force behind them. And the more I've searched, the more evidence I've compiled to make *the case for God*. Within three years of the Russell Burrill seminar I began to find conformational evidence that the Scriptures contained the proof of the existence of God. From my perspective, the scales were tipping in favor of a Creator God. Today, the amount of evidence that I've compiled is overwhelming.

Creation is, in and of itself, the signature of God. God is the only One that can create something from nothing. You've heard the song *"nothing comes from nothing, nothing ever could."*[18] Neither Satan nor all the world's brightest scientists can create life from nothing. A friend of mine worked in Dr. Preston Cloud's laboratory while he was trying to create life from the basic components of matter and energy. Dr. Cloud was unsuccessful. But more to the point, he started with the very matter and energy that had already been brought into existence. Where did the original matter and energy come from? Scientists can't start with

---

18 Sound of Music. Richard Rogers and Oscar Hammerstein. November 1959.

nothing and come up with life. No one ever could and no one ever will. It was confirmation of Peter's cosmological argument.

Sure, scientists can manipulate what God has already created to make hybrid life forms, amalgamated beasts, and clones but we can't create something from nothing. And God's creative work comes in many forms including genetic coding. And those forms came out of nothing but the Word of God. In the beginning, God created the heavens and the earth. He created all that we can see from our planet home, including the plants, animals, and you and me. But even better, from a personal point of view, He has the power to recreate a new heart in an unbeliever like my former self.

Within a few months I was convinced of the existence of God. I was a believer, once the unseen Hand uncovered the embedded code and the chiastic structures that I refer to as wavelengths of literary light. And then there was my discovery of the expanding spiral structure that starts at Genesis and ends at Revelation. I could no longer deny that the Scriptures were authored by a Supernatural Being. How else could any work of literature compiled over a period of more than 1500 years maintain a consistent hidden set of codes and patterns? I was a believer.

Divinely Intertwined Lives

By the time I had my divine appointment with Dr. Peter Stevanoff I had poured through the literature on the subject and scoured the Bible. I had constructed timelines in the lives of dozens of Old Testament heroes. And I had found patterns that form a fabric throughout the Scriptures like chiastic structures, equidistant letter spacing, and the spiral themes that begin as a seed in Genesis and bloom in the book of Revelation. The consistency of the use of the fabric alone points to a supernatural origin. Did each author of the Old Testament know that their writing was a part of a grand weave that went continuously from one end of the Scriptures to the other. I don't see how. So I continued my conversation with Dr. Stevanoff.

I asked metaphorically, "So why not examine the Bible itself to see if the Cross is at the very heart of Infinity?" Peter replied, "Very well Don, where do we start our discussion about your findings?"

"Peter, I want to start with Samson." "Samson? He's an unlikely place to start don't you think?" "Peter, I'm convinced he's the perfect place to start! After all he's one of the best types of Christ that I've found in the Old Testament!" "He hardly seems like a type of Christ to me at all." "Peter, that's just the point. He's the perfect type because he shields the identity of Christ. You might say that he's been hiding the evidence of Christ for such a time as this." "All right Don, I'm all ears. Explain!"

"You see Peter, Samson's life is a near perfect mirror of Christ's life. Their lives connect and intertwine like the strands of DNA. As I proceed, I'll show you that there are more than 52 points that tie the events in the life of Samson to the events in the life of Jesus **in the same time sequence through a mere 96 verses in the account of Samson**.[19] Peter think about it. The life of Samson was constantly guided by an unseen hand. From the visit of the secret angel announcing his birth, to the spirit of the Lord which strengthened him, to the God that sought a chance for him to confront the enemy, Samson was constantly led by a supernatural force. Then Samson sends out the foxes and sets the Philistine fields on fire and of course there's the mystery of the supernatural power in Samson's hair! Both are sold for silver and both of their lives end with their arms outstretched. Peter, that leaves us with a monumental question. Why was the account of Jesus hidden?" Peter looked surprised. "Peter you know the answer. It's the Holy Spirit that covers the Scriptures like a veil and it's the Holy Spirit that can pull back that veil and reveal to us the deeper things of God. In fact, the passage in 1 Corinthians chapter 2 provides the answer." "I know it very well." So Peter turned with me to the passage which says:

But we speak the wisdom of God in a mystery, [even] the hidden [wisdom], which God ordained before the world

---

19 Judges chapters 13 through 16.

> *unto our glory: Which none of the princes of this world knew: <u>for had they known [it], they would not have crucified the Lord of glory</u>. But as it is written, Eye hath not seen, nor ear heard, neither have entered into the heart of man, the things which God hath prepared for them that love him. But God hath revealed [them] unto us by his Spirit: for the Spirit searcheth all things, yea, the deep things of God.[20]*

"So you see Peter, candidly, **if** the Old Testament prematurely revealed the mission of Christ, He would not have been sacrificed on the Cross. His enemies would not have dared to crucify Him. If He had not been sacrificed on the Cross, the Plan of Salvation would have been undermined. Simply put, Jesus was born to die. He was on a mission to rescue the world. His sacrifice is the ultimate representation of the love of God. So **the Plan of Salvation was deliberately hidden through an incredible code** in the Old Testament."   "Don, that's beautiful; it reminds me of John 3:16."

> *For God so loved the world, that he gave his only begotten Son, that whosoever <u>believeth</u> in him should not perish, but have everlasting life. For God sent not his Son into the world to condemn the world; but that the world through him might be saved.[21]*

"Peter, Jesus was born not only to die for you and me, but that the name of God the Father would be vindicated before the entire universe.   The evidence was beautifully hidden behind the *Guardians of God's Secret Code*."

Order of Events to Come

"I'm just curious Don; what cued you into this line of thinking?" "I found several crucial verses that directed my study. Jesus made some outrageous statements that could be Cross-examined. If I

---

20 1 Corinthians 2:7-10.
21 John 3:16, 17.

could prove that Jesus made a false statement, I could throw out the Bible. So I began to pull the string on several of Christ's incredible claims. Christ's key claims are in chapter 24 of Luke."

And beginning at Moses and all the prophets, he expounded unto them in all the scriptures <u>the things concerning himself.</u>[22]

And he said unto them, These [are] the words which I spake unto you, while I was yet with you, that all things must be fulfilled, which were written in the law of Moses, and [in] the prophets, and [in] the psalms, <u>concerning me. Then opened he their understanding, that they might understand the scriptures.</u>[23]

"Jesus boldly claims that the Old Testament was all about Him. How could that be? How could the accounts of characters like Samson, David, Joseph, Joshua, Jonah, Daniel, Esther, and so many others be about Him? How could a worldly being like Samson be about Jesus? My realization was that these characters and ancient accounts could only be about Jesus if *His account was encrypted in theirs*!" "Don, theologians refer to this as typology. Each of the characters that you mention are known as types of Christ. It has been used by scholars for hundreds of years." "Peter, as you'll soon see, my approach is a far deeper application of types." "What's your approach?"

"By comparing the Scriptures *line upon line, precept upon precept*[24] a more complete picture emerges. Therefore, one principle that I've learned for unlocking the hidden code is that the veracity of your conclusions must be based on a comparison of more than one passage. In doing so, you'll arrive at a more comprehensive understanding of the text and assure correct interpretation. In essence, we let the Scriptures serve as their own interpreter." "Sola Scriptura!" "Yes Peter. You might say that our witnesses are *Guardians of God's Secret Code* because they

---

22 Luke 24:27
23 Luke 24:44, 45.
24 Isaiah 28:9, 10.

hid their treasure from unbelievers until the Plan of Salvation had been accomplished."[25] Peter started to get very interested. "What other methods do you apply?" "Scientists refer to the approach that I've been using as an **event sequence analysis**."

"I call the associations "events or links." Links tie Jesus to Old Testament characters like Samson. For example, Samson and Jesus are linked by their names. Samson means *"like the sun"* and by comparison Jesus is called the *"Sun of Righteousness."* Samson is not Jesus, but he's a **type** of Jesus because the events of his life prophetically point to parallel events in the life of Jesus more than a thousand years into the future. Mysteriously, the author of the Scriptures embeds the events in the life of Christ into the historical record of the account of Samson and the lives of a *Great Cloud of Witnesses* throughout the Old Testament." "You're referring to the faith chapter of Hebrews 11." "I assure you it's more than a faith chapter. The cloud of witnesses conceal the evidence." "Interesting concept. What's your basis?"

"When the results of our study are applied to multiple characters we find that likewise, the order of events also occur in the same order as that of the life of Christ." "Incredible Don." "They're more than types of Christ because the correlations extend for two thousand years beyond the life of Christ. His supernatural timeline is defined by the *Plan of Salvation* not just Christ's earthly walk. The events in the lives of the Old Testament characters march in lock-step with the events in the timeline of the Plan of Salvation from the beginning of the Scriptural record to its end; that is, it's a record that extends from before Creation to the end of time." "So you're saying that all these correlations shed more light on the Gospels and His Plan. I'd always thought so. Interesting, very interesting." "Correct Peter. Look at the first point on the scroll of the account of Samson that connects to the life of Jesus."

---

25 Luke 2:6, 21, 22. Luke 18:31. Luke 22:37. John 19:28.

LINK 1: Israel held Captive

"You'll recall Peter, that in the days of Samson,[26] Israel was held captive by the Philistines and was praying for a deliverer. Likewise, in the days of Jesus, Israel was held captive by the Romans. Immediately, we're given a connection between the Israel of Samson and the Israel of Jesus more than a thousand years apart. In both cases, Israel was held in bondage by a foreign power." "Agreed." "It's more than that." "What do you mean?"

"It applies to us today. We live in a world today that's still held captive by a foreign ruler. That foreign ruler is Satan who works through countless fallen angels. We're told that Satan grew envious of Jesus and falsely accused God the Father of establishing a government of Commandments that couldn't be kept. Lucifer's pride[27] caused strife among the angels to such an extent that a war broke out in heaven."

> *And there was war in heaven: Michael and his angels fought against the dragon; and the dragon fought and his angels, And prevailed not; neither was their place found any more in heaven. And the great dragon was cast out, that old serpent, called the Devil, and Satan, which deceiveth the whole world.[28]*

"So you see Peter, from the very beginning of the account of Samson, we see that the message applies to you and me. Satan holds you and I hostage and will rage among mankind until Jesus returns to deliver the Kingdom."

---

26 The events in this chapter are based on Judges Chapter 13.
27 Ezekiel 28:13-18.
28 Revelation 12:7-10.

LINK 2: Angel tells Mother

"Next we see an angel announcing the birth of Samson just as an angel would later announce the birth of Jesus. Mary was a virgin and Samson's mother was barren. From my perspective as a scientist Peter, I don't even know how to quantify the probability of a supernatural appearance of an angel. The recorded appearance of an angel that would announce the births of both Samson and Jesus is an incredibly small happenstance, much less than winning a power ball lottery. So their connections appear to be intentional"

> *And the angel of the LORD appeared unto the woman, and said unto her, Behold now, thou [art] barren, and bearest not: but thou shalt conceive, and bear a son.*[29]

"Peter, in both accounts, Samson's mother and Mary ask the angel how this could be possible. It would have to be a miracle. Neither could bear a child. One was a virgin; the other was barren. By definition that makes them incredible supernatural events."

> *And in the sixth month the angel Gabriel was sent from God unto a city of Galilee, named Nazareth, To a virgin espoused to a man whose name was Joseph, of the house of David; and the virgin's name [was] Mary. And the angel came in unto her, and said, Hail, [thou that art] highly favoured, the Lord [is] with thee: blessed [art] thou among women. And when she saw [him], she was troubled at his saying, and cast in her mind what manner of salutation this should be. And the angel said unto her, Fear not, Mary: for thou hast found favour with God. And, behold, thou shalt conceive in thy womb, and bring forth a son, and shalt call his name JESUS.*[30]

---

29 Judges 13:3.
30 Luke 1:26-31.

ANNOUNCEMENT OF THE MIRACLE BIRTH: Just as the angel Gabriel announced the miracle birth of the Deliverer of Israel so did the Angel, the Secret " I AM" announce the birth of the Deliverer of Israel to the mother of Samson.

LINK 3: Nazarite

"Let's continue Peter. In the account given by Matthew, Jesus is referred to as a Nazarene. Similarly, the angel tells Samson's mother that Samson would be set apart as a Nazarite." We traced the Scriptures in Judges 13:

> *For, lo, thou shalt conceive, and bear a son; and no razor shall come on his head: for the child shall be a <u>Nazarite unto God</u> from the womb:*[31]

"You see Peter, both would be Holy men of God. Samson would be fed physical food for purity. The word *"Nazarite"* is also a term that means *"Branch."* Jesus was the Branch that was cut off (killed) and came back to life (resurrection) just as Aaron's almond rod was cut off, budded, and blossomed. Samson is a Nazarite, by comparison, Jesus is both a Nazarite and a Nazarene. According to the book of Matthew, this fulfilled the words spoken of by the prophets."

> *And he came and dwelt in a city called Nazareth: that it might be fulfilled which was spoken by the prophets, He shall be called a Nazarene.*[32]

LINK 4: Long Awaited Deliverer

Continuing our trace of the Scriptures I said, "In the days of Samson, Israel had been in captivity to the Philistines and the people prayed for a long awaited deliverer."

> *...the child shall be a Nazarite unto God from the womb: and he shall begin to <u>deliver Israel</u> out of the hand of the Philistines.*[33]

---

31 Judges 13:5.
32 Matthew 2:23.
33 Judges 13:5.

"Likewise, in the days of Jesus, Israel had been in captivity to the Romans and was, likewise, praying for a Deliverer."

And so all Israel shall be saved: as it is written, There shall come out of Sion the <u>Deliverer</u>, and shall turn away ungodliness from Jacob: For this [is] my covenant unto them, when I shall take away their sins.[34] And she shall bring forth a son, and thou shalt call his name JESUS: for he shall save his people from their sins.[35]

"Simply put Peter, both Samson and Jesus were born to deliver Israel. The first would physically deliver Israel out of the hands of her earthly captors and the second would deliver Israel out of the hands of her supernatural captors. Both were saviors of Israel." Peter replied with a smile, "And like Samson and Jesus, we have a mission to set the captives of this world free from Satan."

teach all nations, baptizing them in the name of the Father, and of the Son, and of the Holy Ghost[36]

LINK 5: Angel tells Father

"The angel Gabriel came to Joseph in a dream."

… Behold, the angel of the Lord appeared unto him in a dream, saying, Joseph, thou son of David, fear not to take unto thee Mary thy wife: for that which is conceived in her is of the Holy Ghost.[37]

"Likewise, the angel of the LORD appeared to Manoah."

And the angel of the LORD said unto Manoah, Of all that I said unto the woman let her beware. And Manoah said unto the angel of the LORD, I pray thee, let us detain

---

34 Romans 11:26, 27.
35 Matthew 1:21.
36 Matthew 28:19 and 20.
37 Matthew 1:20.

thee, until we shall have made ready a kid for thee. And the angel of the LORD said unto Manoah, Though thou detain me, I will not eat of thy bread: and if thou wilt offer a burnt offering, thou must offer it unto the LORD. For Manoah knew not that he [was] an angel of the LORD.[38]

"Well Peter, that's five connections in a row." "What's next?" "A puzzle!" "What do you mean?" "Peter, who was this Angel?" Peter replied, "I think I know the answer." I smiled in agreement.

LINK 6: the Secret I [Am]

"I think you know the answer too. The angel that brought the message of the miracle birth to Mary and Joseph identified himself as Gabriel, one of two covering cherubs. But the identity of the angel that brought the miracle news of the birth of Samson to Manoah and his wife didn't identify himself by name. In fact he kept it secret." "Who do you think the angel is?" "I think it was Christ. But how did you verify that?"

"The first clue is that the angel identifies himself as I [am]."

And Manoah arose, and went after his wife, and came to the man [the angel], and said unto him, [Art] thou the man that spakest unto the woman? And he said, I [am].[39]

"And in the second clue the angel tells us that His name is a secret." "I think I know where you're going with this Don."

And Manoah said unto the angel of the LORD, What [is] thy name, that when thy sayings come to pass we may do thee honour? And the angel of the LORD said unto him,

---

38 Judges 13:13, 15, 16.
39 Judges 13:11.

JESUS THE SECRET "I AM" announces the miracle birth of Samson, "Like the Sun." Jesus, thus prophesied that Samson would be a Holy One like Himself. As we will see, Samson fulfills his prophetic name step by step in the supernatural path of Jesus.

Why askest thou thus after my name, seeing it [is] secret?[40]

And Manoah said unto the angel of the LORD, What [is] thy name, that when thy sayings come to pass we may do thee honour? And the angel of the LORD said unto him, Why askest thou thus after my name, seeing it [is] secret?[41]

So Manoah took a kid with a meat offering, and offered [it] upon a rock unto the LORD: and [the angel] did wonderously; and Manoah and his wife looked on. For it came to pass, when the flame went up toward heaven from off the altar, that the angel of the LORD ascended in the flame of the altar. And Manoah and his wife looked on [it], and fell on their faces to the ground.[42]

As we continued through the passage, we found that Manoah made a meat offering upon a rock unto the Lord; and *the angel did wondrously*; as Manoah and his wife looked on.

Fire came from the rock, and consumed the sacrifice, and as the flame went up toward heaven …the angel of the Lord ascended in the flame of the altar. And Manoah and his wife looked on it, and fell on their faces to the ground.[43]

"Peter, if Gabriel's name wasn't kept secret, then the Angel that announced the birth of Samson must be an even more important Angel. After all, Gabriel was a covering angel. Manoah knew that they had looked upon the **Holy One of God**, who veiled His glory in the cloudy pillar just as He had in the Pillar Cloud from which He led Israel in the desert. And in the third clue, Manoah realized that he had seen God."

---

40 Judges 13:17, 18.
41 Judges 13:17, 18.
42 Judges 13:19, 20.
43 Judges 13:20.

And Manoah said unto his wife, we shall surely die, because we have seen God. But his wife said unto him, If the LORD were pleased to kill us, he would not have received a burnt offering and a meat offering at our hands, neither would he have showed us all these [things], nor would as at this time have told us [such things] as these.[44]

"Don, theologians refer to the appearance of Christ in the Old Testament as a Theophany.[45] The most stunning appearance of the Son of God is in the fiery furnace with Shadrach, Meshach, and Abednego.[46] Or how about Abraham's three visitors? Two were angels.[47] Jesus was the other. It was Jesus that spoke to Joshua before the battle of Jericho. It was Jesus that spoke to Moses from the pillar cloud that led Israel across the Red Sea." [48]

Moreover, brethren, I would not that ye should be ignorant, how that all our fathers were under the cloud, and all passed through the sea; And were all baptized unto Moses in the cloud and in the sea; And did all eat the same spiritual meat; And did all drink the same spiritual drink: for they drank of that spiritual Rock that followed them: and that Rock was Christ.[49]

"Peter, perhaps none have seen the face of God and lived. But several stood face to face with Jesus, the Son of God."

And the LORD spake unto Moses face to face, as a man speaketh unto his friend. And he turned again into the camp: but his servant Joshua, the son of Nun, a young man, departed not out of the tabernacle.[50]

---

44 Judges 13:22, 23.
45 From the Greek: *Theos* meaning "God" and *Phaneia* meaning "to reveal oneself."
46 Daniel 3:25.
47 Genesis 19:1.
48 SDA Bible Commentary, Volume 2, page 1006.3, 1953.
49 1 Corinthians 10:1-4.
50 Exodus 33:11.

"Jesus explains that He is the image of God the Father."

Jesus saith unto him, Have I been so long time with you, and yet hast thou not known me, Phillip? he that hath seen me hath seen the Father; and how sayest thou [then], Show us the Father?[51]

"Those that saw the face of the Lord saw Jesus and lived. If they had seen the face of God the Father, they would have died because sin cannot come into the presence of God the Father without an intercessor. As Jesus said, *he that hath seen me hath seen the Father*. When anyone came into the presence of the Lord in the Old Testament and lived, they had come into the presence of God the Son not God the Father." "My conclusion exactly Peter. The hidden Jesus of the Old Testament is revealed to us that we would have a basis of faith; not a *leap of faith.*"

Now to him that is of power to stablish you according to my gospel, and the preaching of <u>Jesus Christ, according to the revelation of the mystery, which was kept secret since the world began, But now is made manifest</u>, and by the scriptures of the prophets, according to the commandment of the everlasting God, made known to all nations for the obedience of faith...[52]

LINK 7: Miracle Birth

"Next Peter, we find that Samson is among an elite group of prophesied miracle births in the Scriptures. These miracle births foreshadow and symbolize the birth of Christ." "Good point. I've studied that myself." "How many places in the Scriptures is the birth of a baby boy announced by an Angel first to the mother and then to the father?" "I think I'm catching on. There are two key places: first in the account of Samson in Judges 13, and second at the announcement of the birth of Jesus by the angel Gabriel." "Right Peter. Consider the supernatural announcement of the

51 John 14:9.
52 Romans 16:25, 26.

birth of Isaac, another miracle baby which also leads to one of the most beautiful figures of the Crucifixion of Jesus in the Old Testament."

> *By faith Abraham, when he was tried, offered up Isaac: ...Accounting that God [was] able to raise [him] up, even from the dead; from whence also he received him in a figure.*[53]

"According to the Scriptures, the offering of Isaac was to be understood as a figure of the crucifixion of Jesus. Isaac "acted" as the sacrificial son and Abraham "acted" as the Ancient of Days better *known as God the Father.*" The following provides just a few of the parallels:

- *The births of Isaac and Jesus were announced;*
- *Both are miracle babies;*
- *The story surrounding the sacrifice is a journey of three days;*
- *The sacrifices take place on the same mountain (Moriah);*
- *Both carry the wood for the sacrifice up the hill on their backs;*
- *They assure those with them that they will return;*
- *The sacrifice wears a crown of thorns; and*
- *The Lamb of God is the sacrificial substitute.*[54]

LINK 8: Samson -"Like the Sun"

Peter asked, "What's the next connection?" "The meaning of names in the Scriptures is another key to unlock the hidden messages. For example, the name given to *Lucifer*, which means *Light bearer* was changed to *Satan* meaning *Adversary* because the angel that once stood as a covering cherub accused God and opposed God in warfare. As a consequence, the status of the Covering Cherub fell to sin and was cast from the presence of God.

---

53 Hebrews 11:17-19.
54 Genesis 22:3-18.

BORN AGAIN AS AN OVERCOMER OF SIN: Jacob wrestled with Jesus the "Angel of the Lord" all night and in his wrestling, Jesus changed Jacob's name to "Israel" which means "Overcomer". Jacob was converted as the angel touched his thigh. As we wrestle with the guilt of our sins, Jesus will "*touch our thigh*" and we will be born again.

Hence he was renamed Satan.[55] The name Samson means **Like the Sun** or should we say like the **Son of God**." "The change of the name **Jacob** is of importance to the unlocking the account of Samson. Peter, as Jacob wrestled with the angel of the Lord [Jesus], the angel touched him on the hollow of his thigh and threw it out of joint. The name **Jacob** means **"Usurper or Deceiver"** because he deceived his father and stole the birthright from his brother Esau. Jacob wrestled with the **angel of the Lord** all night and in his wrestling, the angel changed his name to **"Israel"** which means **"Overcomer."** You see, as we wrestle with **Jesus**, the **angel of the Lord**, we take our sin-driven worries to the Lord and He'll forgive us of our sins so that we can overcome them."

And Jacob was left alone; and there wrestled a man with him until the breaking of the day. And when he saw that he prevailed not against him, he touched the hollow of his thigh; and the hollow of Jacob's thigh was out of joint, as he wrestled with him. And he said, Let me go, for the day breaketh. And he said, I will not let thee go, except thou bless me. And he said unto him, What [is] thy name? And he said, Jacob. And he said, Thy name shall be called no more Jacob, but Israel: for as a prince hast thou power with God and with men, and hast prevailed. And Jacob asked [him], and said, Tell [me], I pray thee, thy name. And he said, Wherefore [is] it [that] thou dost ask after my name? And he blessed him there. And Jacob called the name of the place Peniel: for I have seen God face to face, and my life is preserved.[56]

"Like Jacob, Manoah also inquired of the name of the mysterious Angel. It's the Angel Jesus that we must wrestle with that our sins may be forgiven so that you and I can become **Overcomers** or **Israel.** If we are to become sons and daughters of the God of Israel we must wrestle with Jesus that our sins may be forgiven so we can become members of spiritual **Israel.** Whether we are Jew or Gentile, Jesus opens the Door for us to enter into the Kingdom

---

55 Revelation 12:9.
56 Genesis 32:24-30.

of the God of Israel." "But what's the connection to Samson." "You'll have to be patient. The whole account rests on this point."

"And the angel that Jacob wrestled with was Jesus since Jacob saw Him face to face. As in the case of Manoah, Jesus wouldn't reveal His name to Jacob. After Manoah and his wife had come face to face with Jesus, the angel of the Lord, they gave birth to a baby boy that they named **"Samson"**."

> *And the woman bare a son, and called his name Samson: and the child grew, and the LORD blessed him.*[57]

"The literal Samson was not Jesus but the image of the events in the life of Jesus, the **Sun of Righteousness**, are encrypted in the shadows of the account of Samson. And what's amazing is that it was Jesus that announced the birth of Samson as if heralding the coming of His own birth more than a millennium into the future. Was it coincidence that Samson means, **Like the Sun**?"

Event Sequence Analysis

In the first chapter of the account of Samson we see 8 primary events or links that parallel the events in the life of Jesus. The striking realization is that the actions or events are in the same temporal order.

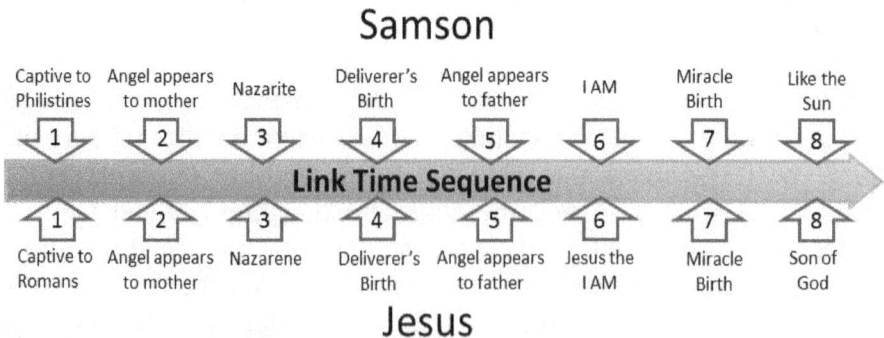

---

57 Judges 13:24.

Probability of 8 Links in a Row

Expressing events in terms of probability provides a means of comparing the scale or likelihood of an event. I use them throughout the book to put things into comparative perspective. We only use probabilities for qualitative comparisons. Many of the events are difficult to realistically estimate a value because they're supernatural. For example, what is the probability that a woman would be visited by an angel to tell her of a future birth? How many births have been announced by an angel throughout history? At best it is a very infrequent occurrence. Yet to provide a compelling conclusion, I try to assign very conservative values throughout the book for each of the links. In this case, I conservatively use 1 in a 100 rather than some difficult to defend number like 1 in a billion or even some larger number.

The event-time sequence of similar parallel events and associations implies a supernatural connection between Samson and Jesus. The parallelism of the first 8 links is beyond coincidence. The ordering of links in the account of Samson is deliberate and is in essence a coded prophecy of the future events in the birth and life account of Jesus. And this coded sequence of events is found in accounts of other Guardians of the secret code.

At the births of Samson and Jesus, Israel was captive to a foreign power. Samson's mother was barren and Mary was a virgin, yet a supernatural being intervened to bring about both miracle births. Both births are prophetically foretold by angels. There've been two recorded times in all of Biblical history that an angel came first to announce the birth of a holy child to the mother followed by an announcement to the father. The connection is unique. We are told that both were chosen, even created by God for a holy mission.

Samson would be a Nazarite; Jesus would be a Nazarite and a Nazarene. The most significant conclusion is that the Angel, the I AM, that announced the birth of Samson is none other than Jesus. Is this mere coincidence? Or if true, then why does Jesus want to bring our attention to the hidden account of Himself embedded within the account of Samson? Could it be to prove that He is the Son of God, the Author and Finisher of our Faith? I'm convinced that the embedded prophecy of Jesus was to provide evidence that Jesus is the Messiah and that God exists.

According to the National Weather Service, the U.S. averages 49 reported lightning fatalities a year which means the odds that you will be struck is less than one in a million or of about the same odds as drawing a royal flush in a single hand or 1.5×10^{-6}. Some estimate the amount of sand on earth's beaches and deserts is roughly 1×10^{18} grains. Finding a single grain blindfolded would be 1×10^{-18}. Others estimate that the odds of Jesus fulfilling eight prophecies of the Old Testament are on the order of 1×10^{-17}. Regardless of the accuracy of these numbers, they are exceptionally small.

To put it bluntly, the likelihood of these eight parallel events occurring in the lives of Samson and Jesus is substantially less than the likelihood of being struck by lightning and may be on the order of finding a single grain of sand in all of Earth's beaches and deserts blindfolded.

As spiritual archaeologists, we've only begun to unearth the event sequence and the evidence will leave you with no other conclusion: God and the realm of the supernatural exist. I've told the account of Samson to numerous audiences, to theologians, pastors, and scientists. It provides incredible evidence of God. We can only conclude that the sequence of events was deliberately encoded hundreds of years in advance of their fulfillment in the account of Jesus by a supernatural Being.

Why was Jesus taking such an integral role in these Old Testament events? Through my research I have concluded that it was Jesus Himself, through the work of the Holy Spirit, that hid the evidence so it would come to Light at the right time.

3 Science in the Cross-hairs

...there shall come in the last days scoffers [some scientists, atheists]...saying, Where is the promise of his [Jesus] coming?... they willingly are ignorant... that by the word of God the heavens were of old, and the earth standing out of the water and in the water: Whereby <u>the world that then was, being overflowed with water [Flood]</u>, perished...[58]

New Orleans was on the horizon as the Amtrak train headed south through the tidal waters surrounding the city. My excitement was building as we neared our final destination. I would be teaching a graduate class at Tulane University in the school of Global Environmental Health. I was looking forward to spending time with my co-chair and our doctoral students. We had been collaborating on an important project for the government. I love working with graduate students. They're challenging to work with but I was well prepared and I would be ready. So I needed to get a good night's sleep so that I would be effective.

As I settled into bed, I couldn't get the code out of my mind. If the code had been in the single isolated case of the account of Samson in the Old Testament, its origin would be difficult enough to explain. But when I realized that the events recorded in the Gospel accounts of the life of Christ are in lock step with the events hidden in the embedded code of numerous Guardians like Samson, I had a dilemma. After years of study I had arrived at the conclusion that the Code had to be embedded by a Being or Beings with a view of events in the past and events in the future. And this Being or these Beings are able to interact, influence, and guide the lives of mankind. The Bible even claims that it was the Lord Himself that was involved in the lives of these Guardians.

---

58 2 Peter 3:3-6.

But his father and his mother knew not that it [was] of the LORD, that he sought an occasion.[59]

No matter how I view the Code, I've never been able to come up with an alternative logical explanation. Could the Bible be true?

After morning classes, I went to lunch with two faculty members to discuss the graduate student projects that we were collaborating on. Our conversation soon drifted to my findings of the code. "Don, how could you believe that the Bible's true?" "James, I was initially trying to disprove the Bible when I started to find ancient codes hidden behind the accounts of the Old Testament characters. Just like you, I was certain that the Bible was authored by men and men alone. But that's all changed." "Why? What could you possibly have found that's so profound that it changed your mind?" "Well take Samson for example. Behind his account I've found numerous links that point to Christ hundreds of years in advance." "Samson? From what I remember, He doesn't have much in common with Christ, does he?" "At first glance, it wouldn't appear so on a superficial reading. But the incredible conclusion is that the coded text prophetically points to nearly 52 key events **in the same temporal order** as it unfolds in the New Testament." "What do you think it means?" "What do you think? The theologians tell me these correlations are types and shadows of Christ. For the most part I agree with the theologians but I assure you, they're far more than types." "Then what are they if they're more than types?" "They're **prophetic evidence** that Christ is the Son of God." "Evidence of the existence of God? You better have more basis than that. Is there anything else?" "Yes, there's a lot more evidence. For example, there are literary patterns much like a poetic framework deliberately incorporated into the Scriptures. The theologians and I agree that the Scriptures are filled with metaphors, chiastic structures, poetry and the like, that many theologians give credit to human authors. I'm convinced the framework is far more than anything that could have been constructed by man alone. This...well... this fabric had to be inserted by a Being outside of time." "Outside of time? You mean

---

59 Judges 14:4.

like God? Why couldn't the ancient text have been dreamt up by men?" "Some patterns cover time frames that extend over hundreds of years. Some longer, even from the beginning to the end of the Scriptures. And the fabric is consistent." "That's interesting."

"It's what I refer to as literary light or illumination. You might say that this fabric is a weave of chiastic structures. And there are different wavelengths of these structures in the form of sine waves embedded throughout the Scriptures." "Are you suggesting that the Words of the Scriptures are giving off light...even energy?" James had a sarcastic grin on his face but his expression changed to amazement when I said, "Take a look at these patterns. What do you think now?" Chemists like James and myself often use light waves as a means of studying the properties and compositions of substances. "I'll admit, that is very surprising...peculiar."

In most scientific circles the discussion of religion is almost taboo but my enthusiasm and my analyses captivated my colleagues. My trip was just beginning to get interesting. But my colleagues would soon make me face the magnitude and seriousness of my conclusions. It put me at odds with science, at least so it would seem superficially. "Don, do you realize the seriousness of your results? Do you realize the implications for your career?"

Science in the Cross-hairs

I nodded and said, "James, it's more serious than you might think. The Scriptures clearly prophesize that scientists will oppose the Bible in the last days. Look at what the text says." As we walked through the following verse, from the book of Second Peter, James became uneasy.

> ***Knowing this first, that there shall come <u>in the last days</u> <u>scoffers, walking after their own lusts</u>, and saying, Where is the promise of his coming? For since the fathers fell asleep, <u>all things continue as [they were] from the beginning</u> of the creation. For this they willingly are***

ignorant of, that by the word of God the heavens were of old, and the earth standing out of the water and in the water: Whereby <u>the world that then was,</u> <u>being</u> <u>overflowed with water,</u> perished... [60]

"Well... I have to admit that these verses clearly warn that in the last days, scientists will openly make fun of the Scriptures. I'm most struck by the fact that the text claims that scientists will scoff at the account of a biblical Flood that covered the world in water."

"James, look again. It says much more than that. It claims that ***all things continue [as they were]***, which is what modern scientists refer to as the theory of uniformitarianism." "James replied, "You're right, I missed that." "Just as the text implies, men today claim that the universe and our spaceship Earth gradually evolved over millions and even billions of years. And they further claim that life sprang forth from the accidental interaction of early constituents in a primordial soup. The Bible prophecy recorded in Second Peter roughly 2000 years ago is being fulfilled today." "I would agree that science today refutes Creation and the Flood of Noah. And science today justifies its claims of the age of the Earth on the basis of the theory of uniformitarianism." "Well then, doesn't it sound to you like the Bible is challenging science to a show-down?"

James and the others that were eavesdropping on our conversation were perplexed. James said, "It all seems too hard to believe...I mean the existence of God." "It did to me at first too. But then there was this evidence. After all, how did the author of the Scriptures know about the paradigm of modern science?" James sighed and said, "Maybe coincidental. Maybe he was being challenged by the Greeks of his day." "He isn't talking about his lifetime. He's pointing to the last days. Surely, the writings of Peter record an amazing set of prophecies that hit at the mainstream of science today. How did he know? Is all this controversy over Creationism versus Science a sign of the end?" I

---

60 2 Peter 3:3-6.

continued to unfold other patterns for their view. They all shook their heads in disbelief.

"James, you know as well as I do that scientists of the stature of Sir Isaac Newton believed in Creation. What happened that changed the *"mind-set"* of so many scientists? The Scriptures self-proclaim that they're of a supernatural origin having been inspired by the Holy Spirit. As far as I'm concerned gentlemen, the evidence that I've found provides scientists with the basis for Cross-examination. These analyses and data show that the Scriptures are tangible, measurable, and subject to investigation." James looked lost in thought and replied softly, "Interesting."

"James, scientists study phenomena, forces, and substances of the natural world that can be measured and examined. Even in the natural world, not all things can be seen, yet their effects can be sensed. Science tells us the universe is made of about 4% normal matter, 21% dark matter, and 74% dark energy.[61] Yet most of the universe is "invisible" to us but we can sense its forces of attraction and repulsion. But of course, the matter and energy that are the building blocks of the universe and life couldn't have come from nothing; nothing ever does. Could it be that the means we use for detection of the supernatural are just as ineffective as our means of studying dark matter and energy?

With this limited understanding of the universe, scientists promote the theory of evolution to explain how you and I arrived on Earth. As a scientific community we fail to examine alternate explanations claimed by the Scriptures. Though science seeks to explain phenomena that we can't explain in the natural world, like dark matter, science avoids delving into the supernatural realm. The Scriptures boldly proclaim that we didn't happen by chance. And perhaps most disconcerting, the Scriptures tell us we're engaged in an unseen war between the forces of Satan and Christ. And most frightening of all, it claims quite literally that these wicked, powerful beings, are wrestling for your soul and mine."

---

61 Energy.gov. *Three ways to bust dark matter*. March 30, 2016.

"Do you have more evidence Don?" "Well James think of it this way. You find 52 points in the lives of Samson and Christ who lived over a thousand years apart...all in the same order." James replied, "I admit, that would be incredible!" "James, more than that, I'm convinced it was deliberate. Explain to me how the author of the 4 chapters of Judges could know about the events in the life of Christ a thousand years in advance?" "What events?" "Well, both Samson and Christ were born when Israel was held captive by a foreign power. Their births were both proclaimed by an angel first to their mothers and then later to their fathers. Both were miracle births. One was the *Sun of Righteousness*, the other is named *Like the Sun*. Both were to be raised as holy children. Both were born to deliver Israel out of the hands of bondage. Both were driven by the Holy Spirit to confront the their captors." "Is that all the proof?" "No, like I said, these parallel events continue for more than 52 points in just 96 verses. It had to be deliberately woven into the account of Samson."

"Are there more parallels?" "Yes, I've found the same time sequence embedded in the accounts of dozens of other characters. What's interesting is that there are gaps deliberately placed in the timeline as you'll learn later. The first scene was about the birth of Samson...or should I say Christ. Then there's a gap. The next scene Samson is all grown up. Likewise, at the same point in the account Jesus goes into the wilderness Temptation." "We need to get back to class but we need to talk. There must be something wrong with all of this. Could we talk more about this at 2:00 in my office" "Sure James, I'd be glad to. I'd like to understand your point of view." I knew then that James was becoming hooked by the evidence. As it was for me, science and God were in opposition in his mind. He wanted to get to the bottom of this, just as I once wrestled with it.

LINK 9: Spirit Drives Him

I met James after class in his office and laid out my analysis of Samson and we resumed our study of the pattern. "What's next?" "Next, both Samson and Jesus were driven by the Spirit to fulfill the mission that they had been given to deliver Israel out of the hands of their captors."

Samson: *And **the spirit of the LORD** began to move him at times in the camp of Dan   between Zorah and Eshtaol.* [62]

Jesus: *Then was Jesus led up of **the Spirit** into the wilderness to be tempted of the devil.* [63]

"You're right.   The   parallel   between   the   two   verses   **is unmistakable.**" "Wait until we get to the verses where Samson releases the foxes and sets the Philistine fields on fire. You'll even be more amazed. Look at our timeline. We've just covered 9 links in a row." "I'm beginning to appreciate your methods. What else have you discovered." "A great deal James!"

LINK 10: Sought the Bride

"Look here! Just as Samson sought a bride, Jesus seeks a spiritual bride worthy of the King of Kings. He seeks His flock, the "*Lost Sheep of Israel*," the symbol of His Bride. And if you search you find that the Scriptures refer to the church as the "*bride*" of Jesus Christ."

> *I will greatly rejoice in the LORD, my soul shall be joyful in my God; for he hath clothed me with the garments of salvation, he hath covered me with the robe of righteousness, as a bridegroom decketh [himself] with ornaments, and as a bride adorneth [herself] with her jewels.* [64]

"Jesus compares His mission to rescue His people through the parable of a wedding feast. His parable of the wedding feast helps us unlock the next few passages about the account of Samson."

---

62 Judges 13:25.
63 Matthew 4:1.
64 Isaiah 61:10.

And Jesus answered and spake unto them again by parables, and said, The kingdom of heaven is like unto a certain king, which made a marriage for his son, And sent forth his servants to call them that were bidden to the wedding: and they would not come. Again, he sent forth other servants, saying, Tell them which are bidden, Behold, I have prepared my dinner: my oxen and [my] fatlings [are] killed, and all things [are] ready: come unto the marriage. But they made light of [it], and went their ways, one to his farm, another to his merchandise: And the remnant took his servants, and entreated [them] spitefully, and slew [them]. But when the king heard [thereof], he was wroth: and he sent forth his armies, and destroyed those murderers, and burned up their city. Then saith he to his servants, The wedding is ready, but they which were bidden were not worthy. Go ye therefore into the highways, and as many as ye shall find, bid to the marriage. So those servants went out into the highways, and gathered together all as many as they found, both bad and good: and the wedding was furnished with guests. And when the king came in to see the guests, he saw there a man which had not on a wedding garment: And he saith unto him, Friend, how camest thou in hither not having a wedding garment? And he was speechless. Then said the king to the servants, Bind him hand and foot, and take him away, and cast [him] into outer darkness; there shall be weeping and gnashing of teeth. For many are called, but few [are] chosen.[65]

"Don, you've got to be able to show me an obvious wedding tie. What is it?" "Well, look here. Jesus went to a wedding at Cana[66] and Samson went to a wedding at Timnath at the same point in the sequence. The lesser would seek a physical bride, the Greater would seek a Spiritual Bride." "Interesting," he said wistfully.

---

65 Matthew 22:1-14.
66 John 2:1.

LINK 11: The Temptation

"If we continue to trace the events in both of their lives, we find that both Samson and Jesus were deliberately moved by the Spirit to confront the powers of their respective world's. Samson was moved to confront the occupying power, the Philistines. Jesus was led by the Spirit to confront the occupying power of Satan and his countless fallen angels that occupy the whole earth." Again I pointed to the two passages:

And Jesus being full of the Holy Ghost returned from Jordan, and was <u>led by the Spirit</u> into the wilderness…[67]

"James, the Spirit filled both Christ and Samson with supernatural power which prepared them for "Spirit" warfare with the enemy. Both would face Satan. They would both face ***temptation*** in the wilderness." "Why the Spirit?" "Once Samson was filled with the Spirit, it ***moved*** him to step out into the world on his own; a step towards the deliverance of Israel. Likewise, Christ was ***moved*** by the Spirit. Samson was moved between Zorah and Eshtaol which has deeper meaning for our study. The same applies to us. Look at the verse."

And the <u>spirit of the LORD</u> began <u>to move him at times</u> in the <u>camp of Dan</u> between <u>Zorah</u> and <u>Eshtaol</u>.[68]

In the Hebrew, the "***camp of Dan***" means under the "***banner or place*** of ***judgment***." You could say that both were in a personal trial. You could say that the actions of Jesus and Samson were tested and judged based on their actions. Both had freedom of choice to either fall to the flesh or walk with the spirit." "So you look at the original meaning in the Hebrew text?" "If you don't, you miss a lot of the original meaning. For example, the Hebrew for "***at times***" can be translated to "***stir up or agitate***." Samson's mind was being agitated to confront the enemy. You might say he

---

67 Luke 4:1.
68 Judges 13:25.

was struggling between the mission given to him by God and the lust of the flesh."

"In the Hebrew, the word *"Zorah"* means *"hornet"* which can wound or kill its victim with a sting. It has carnal implications. In opposition, the Hebrew word *"Eshtaol"* has a pleading (humble request) connotation meaning *"entreaty"* or *"fervent prayer"*."

"Christ overcame the **temptations of the flesh** that Satan was tempting Him with by remaining in constant communication with God the Father through fervent prayer. At His baptism, the dove descended upon Jesus as God the Father announced *"this is my Son in whom I am well pleased."* You might say that Jesus was filled with the Spirit to over-flowing. God the Father was announcing the beginning of the mission of His Son to confront the enemy and take back planet Earth."

"Jesus tells us that we can receive the Holy Ghost just as the apostles did at Pentecost. Samson had choices, just like we do to overcome the **temptations of the flesh**. Like Samson, you and I can move against the enemies of this world with the power of the Holy Spirit. For we defeat the enemy *not by might, nor by power, but by my spirit, saith the LORD of hosts.*[69]"

LINK 12: Confront the Enemy

"Jesus and Samson were both driven by supernatural agencies to confront the enemy. Those surrounding Jesus and Samson didn't know that it was the Spirit that drove them to their encounters." Of Samson we're told:

> *But his father and his mother knew not that it [was] of the LORD, that he sought an occasion against the Philistines: for at that time the Philistines had dominion over Israel.*[70]

---

69 Zechariah 4:6.
70 Judges 14:4.

"The Scriptures clearly state that it was **the Lord that was the force that caused Samson to confront the enemy**. Likewise, **it was the Holy Spirit that strengthened Jesus to confront the enemy**." "But why?" "It was all a part of a greater Plan...we'll get there." "Strengthened by the Spirit?" "Jesus maintained a constant connection with God the Father through fervent prayer and the power of the Spirit. Imagine! Christ's body was in a pitiful and weakened state by forty days of denying the lusts of the flesh. After forty days, His body was screaming out for food but Jesus placed humanity's needs above His own as a demonstration of His love. No human being could starve and yet live forty days without supernatural intervention and the Spirit that filled Jesus gave Him the strength to live. You might say that Jesus ate the Word of God which is the bread of life. So when Satan approached Jesus in His emaciated human state and said, ***"If thou be the Son of God, command this stone that it be made bread. Jesus replied saying, "It is written, That men shall not live by bread alone, but by every word of God."*** [71]"

"Jesus was tempted by Satan just as you and I are, yet He didn't fall to sin. And although Satan relentlessly assailed Him with fleshly tests of appetite, lust for power, and ambition, Jesus succeeded by defeating Satan with the Word of God."

> ***For the word of God [is] quick, and powerful, and sharper than any two-edged sword, piercing even to the dividing asunder of soul and spirit, and of the joints and marrow, and [is] a discerner of the thoughts and intents of the heart.*** [72]

LINK 13: Defeats the Lion

"Don, show me the next obvious connection." "All right James, in the parallel case, the Holy Spirit within Samson moved him to go forth from the nurturing of his parents into a world filled with sin

---

71 Matthew 4:3, 4.
72 Hebrews 4:12.

and violence. Samson had been raised as a Nazarite and trained as a soldier of God. It was now time for Samson to be used by the Spirit to begin his mission of the liberation of Israel." "Are you inferring that Samson was somehow supposed to be Christ?" "Good question James. Samson's not Jesus Christ but he was deliberately selected as were many of the other characters of the Old Testament to serve as a living prophecy of the real Redeemer and Deliverer of Israel, Jesus Christ. And so it was that Samson was destined to confront the lion that roared against him." "How does that connect Samson to Jesus?" "You could say that as the mission of Jesus heated up, those in opposition to Him roared as a lion. The people were stirred by Satan and the fallen angels to speak out against Jesus. The more Jesus showed His power in being able to heal the sick, raise the dead, and cast out demons, the more the screaming of the people increased until at the last, the evil spirits led by Satan caused the crowds to scream out, *Crucify Him! Crucify Him!* Pilate and the people knew that Jesus was innocent and undeserving of being crucified, but the fallen angels entered into the people and took over their bodies, causing them to cry out, *Crucify Him! Crucify Him!*" "James, you can't withstand Satan alone. Jesus confronted Satan in the wilderness after being filled by the Holy Spirit. He used the Words of the Scriptures as His defense. In the Book of Hebrews it says,

> *By faith the harlot Rahab perished not with them that believed not, when she had received the spies with peace. And what shall I more say? for the time would fail me to tell of Gedeon, and [of] Barak, and [of] Samson, and [of] Jephthae; [of] David also, and Samuel, and [of] the prophets: Who through faith subdued kingdoms, wrought righteousness, obtained promises, stopped the mouths of lions..."* [73]

"Did you get that James? He stopped their mouths...the Scribes and Pharisees were dumbfounded at the teachings of Jesus... And later the Scriptures show once again, the power of the WORDs of Christ over Satan..."

---

[73] Hebrews 11:31-33.

WILDERNESS LION IS A SYMBOL OF SATAN: Samson defeated the physical lion in the wilderness just as Jesus defeated Satan the supernatural "roaring lion."

"The Power of Christ over Satan was in the WORD."

And the devil said unto him, All this power will I give thee, and the glory of them: for that is delivered unto me; and to whomsoever I will I give it. If thou therefore wilt *worship me, all shall be thine. And Jesus answered and said unto him, <u>Get thee behind me, Satan:</u> for it is written, Thou shalt worship the Lord thy God, and him only shalt thou serve.*[74]

"First Peter tells you that you should: ***<u>Be sober, be vigilant; because your adversary the devil, as a roaring lion, walketh about, seeking whom he may devour...</u>***"[75]

"Samson would head out from home, driven by the Spirit, and like Christ, Samson would be confronted by the roaring lion."

Then went Samson down, and his father and his mother, to Timnath, and came to the vineyards of Timnath: and, behold, <u>a young lion roared against him.</u>[76]

LINK 14: Honey

"The Bible's clear that you and I won't enter heaven without trials and tribulations. As long as you and I walk the face of this earth we'll be caught up in the warfare between Christ and Satan." I pointed James to the scripture where it says:

For we wrestle not against flesh and blood, but against principalities, against powers, against the rulers of the darkness of this world, against spiritual wickedness in high [places].[77]

"You mean there's no escape?" "Christ has made a way of escape. Christ provides us with the key to make our escape. So does Samson as a shadow of Christ." "But how?"

"As Samson continued on his mission to find a bride, he went back to the carcass of the lion. And when he arrived he found honey in

---

74 Luke 4:6-8.
75 1 Peter 5:8.
76 Judges 14:5.
77 Ephesians 6:12.

the remains of the dead lion. If we pull the golden thread on the word "*honey*" by searching elsewhere in the Scriptures, we find that the Word of God is as honey; even sweeter than honey." "Honey?" "Yes honey! Because of sin we're destined to wage continual warfare against Satan and his evil spirits. Christ defeated Satan by quoting the honey of the spirit, the Word of God."

> *How sweet are thy words unto my taste! [yea, sweeter] than honey to my mouth! Through thy precepts I get understanding: therefore I hate every false way. Thy word [is] a lamp unto my feet, and a light unto my path.*[78]

"You see James, within the body of the dead lion, Samson found the honey that symbolizes the Word of God. And it was the Word of God that was used by Christ to defeat Satan, the roaring lion. The Word of God penetrated the mind of Satan as a sword."

> *For the word of God [is] quick, and powerful, and sharper than any two-edged sword, piercing even to the dividing asunder of soul and spirit, and of the joints and marrow, and [is] a discerner of the thoughts and intents of the heart.*[79]

"You might say that the Word of God is a supernatural weapon that can fend off the devil and his fallen spirits. If we would but seek God in His Word and summon Him through prayer we would find that His angels are all around us."

> *"Are they not all ministering spirits, sent forth to minister to those who shall be heirs of salvation?"*[80]

"I'm sorry James, we'll have to pick this up later. I've got a class to teach."

---

78 Psalms 119:101-105.
79 Hebrews 4:12.
80 Hebrews 1:14.

Event Sequence Analysis

In Judges Chapter 13 we saw 8 primary links that parallel the events in the life of Jesus. Again we find that the temporal sequence of events continue as we move through Chapter 14 of the Book of Judges.

Both were to be Deliverers of Israel. The first was sent to deliver physical Israel, the second was sent to deliver Spiritual Israel. Both sought a bride. Samson sought a physical Bride. Jesus sought the spiritual bride. And Jesus continues to seek that bride today. Both would confront the enemy. The first was guided to confront the Philistines. The second would confront Satan's unseen kingdom. The first defeats a roaring lion whereas; the second defeats Satan the roaring lion. Samson finds honey in the carcass of the dead lion. Jesus would defeat Satan, the roaring lion, with the spiritual honey that we refer to as the Word of God.

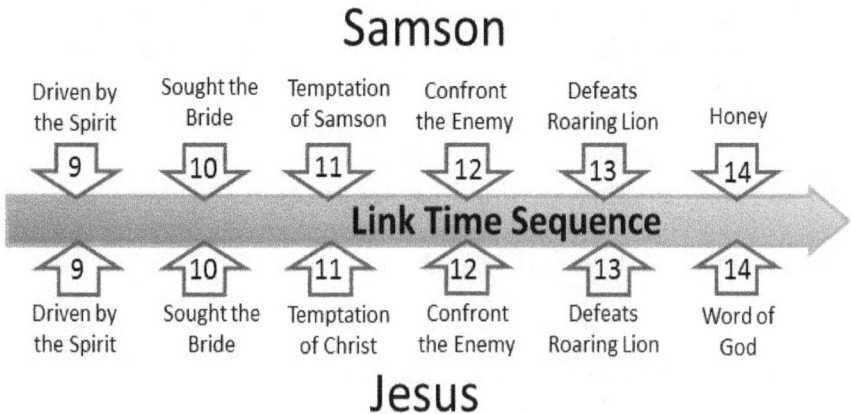

Samson

Driven by the Spirit	Sought the Bride	Temptation of Samson	Confront the Enemy	Defeats Roaring Lion	Honey
9	10	11	12	13	14

Link Time Sequence

9	10	11	12	13	14
Driven by the Spirit	Sought the Bride	Temptation of Christ	Confront the Enemy	Defeats Roaring Lion	Word of God

Jesus

14 Links in a Row

There are on the order of 10^{19} grains of sand on earth's beaches and deserts. The probability of fourteen events in a row are on the order of you finding a single grain of sand hidden among all the grains of sand on the beaches and deserts of planet Earth while you are blind-folded!

4 *Wedding Riddles*

James' curiosity was piqued by our conversations and several days later he took me to a restaurant overlooking Lake Pontchartrain. In the distance we could see the lights of the city across the shore. And once again our conversation shifted to my studies on the Scriptures. "Do you realize the significance of your findings? Seriously Don, do you know what this means if you publish your results?" "James, I know how Rips was severely criticized by the scientific community for his Bible Code. His critics say that he lacks objectivity. I know I'm gonna face the same scrutiny." "Don, you need to be sure, very sure."

"James I've studied the Scriptures from every possible angle. I've applied my approach to more than twenty character studies in the Old Testament. All of my results are consistent. As far as I'm concerned there's no doubt about the hidden code. If I'd only found the pattern behind a single character my claims might be different. But I find consistency in the patterns everywhere."

"Are you sure…I mean, are you really confident that your findings are reproducible. What if other investigators don't agree with your findings?" James stared at me waiting for the answer. We both knew that the implications were difficult to comprehend.

"James, the scientific community is full of disagreements. It's time to put my findings in print. And yes, I'm very certain." "Can your results be reproduced?" "Yes, I'm sure that they can." Then James asked the big questions.

"If what you've found is true then how can you reconcile the Flood with what we know about geology today? And there's that little enormous obstacle of the age of the earth. How can you possibly reconcile science with the Scriptural statements?" "My doubting Thomas concluded that if God exists He can do anything. James, I know that's not the answer you're looking for because I've wrestled with the same questions." "So how do you answer the concerns scientists have raised about a world-wide Flood?" I'm addressing these issues in a book I'm currently writing[81] but for now James, you deserve an answer. There are rock formations called turbidites found all around the world." "Turbidites?" "They're sediments that are deposited rapidly underwater by a flood. They're thought to be mudslides that cascade off the continental shelves triggered by earthquakes. They're famous for cutting the trans-Atlantic cables.[82] They can cross oceans. They provide the explanation of how rock formations like the Tapeats sandstone can extend from Canada and the eastern U.S. to the Grand Canyon. How do you explain the rapid deposition of a single rock formation that can cover continents any other way?[83] And then of course there are salt formations scattered across the United States from Syracuse New York, Michigan, even to the Great Salt Lake of Utah and Deaf Smith County in Texas. And then what about the presence of numerous fossil beds where the victims were apparently buried alive. These fossil beds are found world-wide." "What about the mountains?" "Perhaps the mountains and even the break-up of Pangea could have accompanied events surrounding the Flood."[84] "Don, I can imagine numerous local floods but a single world-wide flood?" "James there is plenty of evidence of worldwide flooding. Besides I can't explain my data and analyses from the Scriptures any other way." "Well, how do you justify the vast differences in time between the Scriptures and geologic time?" "Again James, I don't pretend to have all the answers. But God's time isn't our time. God exists outside of our time and He sees the end from the beginning. Take a look at the Scriptures. Maybe some of the references to time in the Scriptures are in God's reference of time, not ours?"

[81] Alexander, D.H. 2020. Apocalypse Now: The Rocks Cry Out. Sword Bearers Ministry.
82 Julia Rosen. Nov. 18, 1929: The Day the Cables Broke. Nov. 20, 2013. VisionLearning.
83 Chadwick, A.V. and M.E. Kennedy. Depositional Environment of the Tapeats Sandstone in the Region of the Grand Canyon, Arizona. Geoscience Research Institute, Loma Linda, California 92350. 2001.
84 Earth in Upheaval. Immanuel Velikovsky. 1956. Doubleday. New York.

POWER OF SAMSON: GUARDIAN OF GOD'S SECRET CODE

But, beloved, be not ignorant of this one thing, that one day [is] with the Lord as a thousand years, and a thousand years as one day.[85]

"And James, that having been said, there's the question about the second verse of the Book of Genesis. It doesn't rule out an ancient earth without form. The formless earth could have been created long before the account of the creation week."

And the earth was without form, and void; and darkness [was] upon the face of the deep.[86]

"James, I don't have all the answers. But I do know this. The Scriptures provide the evidence in a way that's reproducible by independent researchers." "You need more to go on Don. What about the age of the universe. It's based on the speed of light?" "I've thought about that too James. The Bible provides an answer. It says in many places, **thus saith God the LORD, he that created the heavens, and stretched them out.**[87] If God said it, I believe it." "That's an interesting thought about light being stretched. That would certainly change our understanding of time." "James, as you study my findings, I'm confident that you'll arrive at the same conclusions I have. I'm certain that the hidden code in the Scriptures are deliberately embedded by some Being or Beings that could see a thousand years and more into the future." "Don, c'mon. Are you really suggesting that this guy Rips actually stumbled onto a hidden mathematical code that has a supernatural origin?" "Maybe he has James. I've studied his works. His critics say that his patterns are found in other works of literature...even Moby Dick. But I wouldn't discount his work just yet." "How's your code any different?"

"The patterns that I've found are everywhere in the Scriptures and they're consistent, like a signature of the Author. Rips work focused on the Torah. And Rips work isn't new. Sir Isaac Newton

---

85 2 Peter 3:8.
86 Genesis 1:2.
87 Isaiah 42:5.

found symbolic language throughout the Scriptures based upon his studies of the books of Daniel and The Revelation of John. Imagine what Newton would have found with a computer. Newton's studies served as my inspiration to dig into the use of figurative language to unlock the Scriptures."

Newton's Bible Code[88]

"In 1958, Rabbi Weissmandel found a *"Bible Code*." He found that the four letters of the Hebrew word (תּוֹרָה) translated as TORAH in English occur at a 50 letter count interval starting in Genesis and ending in the middle of the Book of Leviticus without a computer. He lost the trail for a while but later realized that the Hebrew word for TORAH was spelled backwards from that point and ends in the Book of Deuteronomy." The expression on James face shifted to that look of amazement. "Amazingly, Sir Isaac Newton searched the Bible for codes in the Old Testament in an effort similar to mine." "A scientist like Newton?" I replied, sarcastically, "Of course, Newton had to master Hebrew to crack the codes! Weissmandel used intense manual methods of study that can now be mastered by Bible code software of equidistant letter spacing (ELS). Is this numerical literary fabric the signature of God or an ancient writing style? Weissmandel thought it was the signature of God and so do some modern Bible code researchers. Or is *"Bible Code"* simply a

---

88 This a copy of a painting by Sir Godfrey Kneller(1689). This copy was painted by Barrington Bramley. Institute for Mathematical Sciences, University of Cambridge. Public domain.

statistical oddity? Or was it a style that Moses learned in the Pharaoh's court?" I showed James the image below that shows the Hebrew four letter word for Torah at a 50 letter interval.[89] As seen in this figure, Hebrew word (תּוֹרָה) is circled:

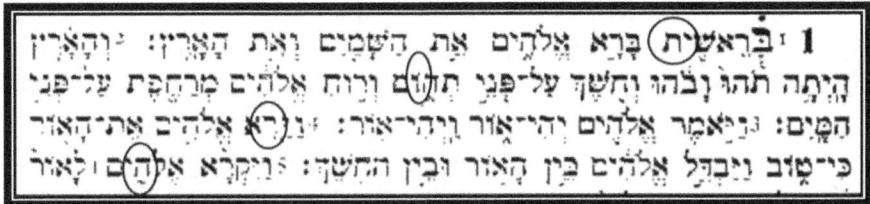

"James, many other researchers like Drosnin and Witzum, Rips, and Rosenberg[90] are convinced that the ELS code is of a meta-physical origin. But according to modern scholars, the number code in the structure of the Torah was adapted as a compositional style for structuring the text by the ancient scribes in a manner befitting the sacredness of the masterpiece. Who's right?

It appears that the biblical text was composed according to preconceived models and patterns shaped by certain numbers that regulate the amount of words, sentences, and verses. Specific numbers were used to forge the structure of the text in its different component parts. Like musical compositions, which are artistically constructed and arranged with the help of rhythm and melody, so literary texts in biblical antiquity were composed and structurally organized with the help of certain numbers. In short, the art of writing practiced by the biblical writers seems to have involved compositional techniques inextricably bound up with counting.[91]

James replied, "Very interesting."

---

89 Bible Code in Genesis 1:1-4. 1909 . Public domain.
90 Witzum , D., Rips, E. and Rosenberg, Y. (1994) Ibid.
91 Labuschagne, C.J. *Numerical Secrets of the Bible: Rediscovering the Bible Codes.* (2000). Bible Press, N. Richland Hills, TX. Page 1 of 192 pages.

"James, could the construction of the Scriptures have been guided by an unseen Hand? Newton thought so. So do I. Newton spent as much time studying the Bible as he spent on science. Newton discovered that the Bible uses symbolic language. He wrote a treatise on the prophetic books of ***Daniel and Revelation***. According to Newton,[92] although Daniel lived in the time of Babylon, the prophecies given to him by the angel Gabriel accurately record the rise and fall of kingdoms, hundreds of years into the future." And I continued, knowing that James was intrigued. "And Newton's work convinced me that the Beasts that I saw on the screen years earlier weren't really beasts at all. They're symbols of world powers."

> ***The ram which thou sawest having [two] horns [are] the kings of Media and Persia and the rough goat [is] the king of Grecia...***[93]

"James, how could anyone read the dreams of another without supernatural help? How could anyone accurately predict the rise and fall of future kingdoms without supernatural eyes?" Once I reviewed Newton's discoveries, I decided I'd better investigate further! After all, Newton is credited with the development of integral calculus. Newton understood the Biblical characters to be symbols. That was a key for me. The Bible is written in symbolic language. If scientists like Newton and Einstein maintained a deep interest in the Bible for decades, then the Bible is no ordinary book." "But are your findings the same as the works of Newton or Rips?" "My ***event sequence analysis*** is based on Newton's approach; not ELS. The patterns that I've found stand on their own merit. Think about it. Samson's birth was announced by an angel to his mother. Later the angel confirmed the birth to his disbelieving father. In parallel, the birth of Christ was announced first to Mary and then to Joseph. Both Samson and Jesus were driven into the wilderness. Both experienced temptation. Their enemies plotted to trap and kill them. They were both sold for silver and captured. One was blinded. The other was blindfolded.

---

92 Newton, Isaac, Sir. Daniel and the Apocalypse. J. Murray London. 1922.
93 Daniel 8:20, 21.

Both were made fun of and paraded around by a murderous crowd. And both Samson and Jesus ended their lives with arms outstretched."

> **Strong's Lexicon 02420 chiydah {khee-daw'} AV - riddle 9, dark sayings 3, hard question 2, dark sentence 1, proverb 1, dark speech 1; 17 1) riddle, difficult question, parable, enigmatic saying or question, perplexing saying or question 1a) riddle (dark obscure utterance) 1b) riddle, enigma (to be guessed) 1c) perplexing questions**

"Don, what are you concluding that your results mean?" I replied emphatically, "All I can figure is that *Some Being, the One we call God, is providing evidence that He exists.*"

Parables[94], Riddles, Metaphors

"James, the art of the riddle is a brain tease designed to maintain your attention for days, months, even years. It could even be used to mesmerize you. Riddles and parables are literary means of captivating and maintaining your attention by setting forth a fascinating puzzle." "Why not be direct?"

"A riddle sets *a nail in a sure place.*[95] Some riddles are meant to be easily understood and others are meant to be hidden and kept secret except from the most diligent seekers. Jesus kept many things veiled from the masses so that His Plan of Salvation would succeed." I pointed James to the following text:

> *All these things spake Jesus unto the multitude in parables; and without a parable spake he not unto them: That it might be fulfilled which was spoken by the prophet, saying, I will open my mouth in parables; I will*

---

94 Matthew 13:34.
95 Isaiah 22:23.

utter things which have been kept secret from the foundation of the world.[96]

"Unbeknownst to the Scribes and Pharisees, each event in the life of Jesus unlocked the secrets of the Old Testament. Each event was the fulfillment of multiple hidden prophecies concerning Him. Even the Exodus walk of Moses and Israel were given to us as examples."

Now all these things happened unto them for ensamples: and they are written for our admonition, upon whom the ends of the world are come.[97]

LINK 15: Two Weddings

"James, in the Old and New Testaments, the wedding of a bride and bridegroom represents the sacred union between Christ and His people. That is, the woman represents the Church. And the Church is the bride of Christ. **Samson attends his wedding at Timnath** at the beginning of his mission to free Israel and similarly **Jesus attends the wedding at Cana** at the beginning of His earthly ministry to free Israel." "That's straightforward."

"Samson went with his parents down to Timnath to seek a bride. And as was the custom, Samson prepared a feast. Thus, Samson symbolizes the bridegroom and the woman that Samson sought represents a church."

*So his father went down unto the woman: and **Samson made there a feast**; for so used the young men to do.*[98]

"Like Samson, Christ will prepare a banquet for His bride, a feast referred to as the *"marriage supper of the Lamb."* One would free Israel from the bondage of the Philistines, the other would free Israel from the bondage of the grave."

---

96 Matthew 13:34, 35.
97 1 Corinthians 1:11.
98 Judges 14:10.

"The bride of Christ is symbolized as a woman clothed with the Sun. In other words, the rays of Christ, the Sun of Righteousness, totally encompass her as a robe of light. Her feet are set upon the moon, meaning that she walks totally within the confines of the Word of God which provides her divine illumination."

> **_Bride of Christ_: _And there appeared a great wonder in heaven; a woman clothed with the sun, and the moon under her feet, and upon her head a crown of twelve stars_.**[99]

"What about Satan's bride?" "Good question James. As contrasted with the Bride of Christ, Satan's bride is characterized as a group of followers that are living in a fallen state."

> **_Bride of Satan_: _I saw a woman sit upon a scarlet coloured beast, full of names of blasphemy, having seven heads and ten horns. And the woman was arrayed in purple and scarlet colour, and decked with gold and precious stones and pearls, having a golden cup in her hand full of abominations and filthiness of her fornication: And upon her forehead [was] a name written, MYSTERY, BABYLON THE GREAT, THE MOTHER OF HARLOTS AND ABOMINATIONS OF THE EARTH. And I saw the woman drunken with the blood of the saints, and with the blood of the martyrs of Jesus..._**[100]

"Satan's bride is adorned in worldly clothing. She's clothed in purple and scarlet, wearing jewelry of precious stones and pearls and holding a cup full of abominations. Symbolically, she's drunken or deluded with a doctrine that causes the death of the Saints. In a spiritual context, sin is the cause of the death of the Saints, for *the wages of sin is death*."

---

99 Revelation 12:1.
100 Revelation 17:3-6.

LINK 16: Wedding Invitation

"James, at the wedding, Samson's father *invites* "*companions*" to the wedding banquet. Similarly, God the Father is inviting each of us, whether of the fold or of the highways and the by-ways to the wedding." I returned to the parable of the marriage of the King's Son to put the invitation in context and set up the next points.

> *the kingdom of heaven is like unto a certain king, which made a marriage for his son, and sent forth his servants to call them that were bidden to the wedding: and they would not come. Again, he sent forth other servants, saying, Tell them which are bidden, Behold, I have prepared my dinner: my oxen and [my] fatlings [are] killed, and all things [are] ready: come unto the marriage. But they made light of [it], and went their ways, one to his farm, another to his merchandise: and the remnant took his servants, and entreated [them] spitefully, and slew [them]. But when the king heard [thereof], he was wroth: and he sent forth his armies, and destroyed those murderers, and burned up their city. Then saith he to his servants, The wedding is ready, but they which were bidden were not worthy. Go ye therefore into the highways, and as many as ye shall find, bid to the marriage. So those servants went out into the highways, and gathered together all as many as they found, both bad and good: and the wedding was furnished with guests. And when the king came in to see the guests, he saw there a man which had not on a wedding garment: And he saith unto him, Friend, how camest thou in hither not having a wedding garment? And he was speechless. Then said the king to the servants, Bind him hand and foot, and take him away, and cast [him] into outer darkness; there shall be weeping and gnashing of teeth. For many are called, but few [are] chosen.*[101]

---

101 Matthew 22:2-14.

"James, we see two important keys to unlocking Samson's account through the parable of the Wedding of the King's Son:

First Key: we see that the invitation of the King, none other than God the Father, is rejected by those that were first invited. So the King determines them to be unworthy. Therefore, God the Father goes to the highways to invite all who will be drawn by the love of His Son. The application's clear. As Jesus told the parable to the Pharisees and Sadducees, they knew that Jesus was speaking of their rejection. They couldn't accept Jesus as the Son of the King because He didn't fill their paradigm. Likewise, Jesus tells the Jewish leaders that if they reject Him, His Father will take the wedding invitation to the highways and give the invitation to the Gentiles, both good and bad. Plainly, He's saying that all are invited to the Kingdom." "What's the next key?" The **Second Key** is that those without a wedding garment will be bound and cast into outer darkness. Unfortunately, they'll be lost forever."

LINK 17: Two Riddles

"So what's the lesson of the wedding garments?" "Both Samson and Jesus give a riddle! Samson gives a riddle of the garments to his companions at the same point that Jesus gives a riddle to Nicodemus." "That is an interesting connection. What do they have in common?"

"Both riddles given by Samson and Jesus were about wedding garments." "Wedding garments?" "Yes, wedding garments."

Samson's Riddle of the Garments

James looked perplexed, so I continued. "Samson set forth a riddle as a bet. He was certain that the thirty companions that his father had gathered could not solve it during the seven days of the wedding feast. And so Samson promised them a change of garments if they could solve the riddle. If Samson lost he would have to buy them each a change of garments."

> *And Samson said unto them, I will now put forth a riddle unto you: if ye can certainly declare it me within the seven days of the feast, and find [it] out, then I will give you thirty sheets and thirty change of garments: But if ye cannot declare [it] me, then shall ye give me thirty sheets and thirty change of garments. And they said unto him, Put forth thy riddle, that we may hear it. And he said unto them, <u>Out of the eater came forth meat, and out of the strong came forth sweetness.</u> And they could not in three days expound the riddle.*[102]

"But the companions threatened the bride to get Samson to disclose the riddle or they would burn his bride and her Father. So Samson's Philistine wife wept and begged him for seven days to tell her the answer. And finally Samson revealed the riddle to her. And so she betrayed him and told the companions the riddle. And as it is recorded, *the men of the city said unto him on the seventh day before the sun went down, What [is] sweeter than honey? and what [is] stronger than a lion? And he said unto them, If ye had not plowed with my heifer, ye had not found out my riddle.*"[103] "What does it mean?" "To the question, "*What is sweeter than honey?*" We know that the deeper answer is the *Word of God.* And to the question, "*What is stronger than a lion?*" We know that *Jesus the Lion of the Tribe of Judah* is more powerful than Satan, the roaring lion. But there remains yet a deeper and far more important hidden message." James continued to look puzzled.

Christ's Riddle of the Garments

"Look James, like Samson, at the parallel point in the two accounts, Jesus gives a riddle of the wedding garments. Nicodemus, a Pharisee, thought that there was credibility to Christ's teachings because of the miracles he had witnessed. And so one evening, under the cover of darkness, Nicodemus made his

---

102 Judges 14:12-14.
103 Judges 14:18.

way to a clandestine meeting with the Master. But Jesus read his mind and his heart. Jesus knew that Nicodemus was a believer and his heart was ready for conversion. And so Jesus told Nicodemus that he must be born again. But Nicodemus didn't understand the metaphor. The concept was foreign to him." We're told that:

> *Jesus answered and said unto him, Verily, verily, I say unto thee, Except a man be born again, he cannot see the kingdom of God. Nicodemus saith unto him, How can a man be born when he is old? can he enter the second time into his mother's womb, and be born? Jesus answered, Verily, verily, I say unto thee, Except a man be <u>born of water and [of] the Spirit</u>, he cannot enter into the kingdom of God.*[104]

"Don, what does this all mean? And how does it explain Samson's riddle?" "It begs the question of what holds humanity back from seeing the deeper meanings of the Scriptures. It's their unbelief in Jesus and His power to save us. You see James, we must be born again and put on garments of salvation." I turned to the following passage:

> *I will greatly rejoice in the LORD, my soul shall be joyful in my God; for he hath clothed me with the <u>garments of salvation</u>, he hath covered me with the robe of righteousness, as a bridegroom decketh [himself] with ornaments, and as a bride adorneth [herself] with her jewels.*[105]

You Must Be Born Again

"James, baptism isn't the simple act of being dunked in water. It's the conscious choice of accepting Jesus as your Savior. You must give up your life of sin and start a new life as a believer. Let's continue." And as Jesus continued to explain to Nicodemus,

---

104 John 3:3-5.
105 Isaiah 61:10.

whosoever believeth in him should not perish, but have eternal life. For God so loved the world, that he gave his only begotten Son, that whosoever believeth in him should not perish, but have everlasting life. For God sent not his Son into the world to condemn the world; but that the world through him might be saved.[106]

"Note here James that immediately after Christ's discussion with Nicodemus we read, *After these things came Jesus and his disciples into the land of Judaea; and there he tarried with them, and baptized. And John also was baptizing in Aenon near to Salim, because there was much water there: and they came, and were baptized.*[107] Baptism was central to the riddle that Jesus gave to Nicodemus, for shortly after their meeting **both** Jesus and John went to the land of Judaea to baptize those that were new believers and give them change of garments!" "But what is the wedding garment?" "Jesus is said to wear a garment of light." As it is recorded: *Who coverest [thyself] with light as [with] a garment: who stretchest out the heavens like a curtain…*[108]"If we continue to examine the parable of the Wedding of the King's Son you'll understand."

And when the king came in to see the guests, he saw there <u>a man which had not on a wedding garment</u>: And he saith unto him, Friend, <u>how camest thou in hither not having a wedding garment?</u> And he was speechless. Then said the king to the servants, Bind him hand and foot, and take him away, and cast [him] into outer darkness; there shall be weeping and gnashing of teeth. For many are called, but few [are] chosen.[109]

"A *<u>change of garment</u>* is the requirement to get into Christ's wedding. You must accept Jesus as the King's Son." "So does that mean that only few will be in heaven? Does that mean that my case is hopeless?" "Not at all! Don't be discouraged even though

---

106 John 3:15-17.
107 John 3:22, 23.
108 Psalm 104:2.
109 Matthew 22:11-14.

Satan and his evil spirits are causing you great tribulation. Jesus tells us that all we need to do is believe in Him." As summed up in the writings of John:

> ***But these are written, that ye might believe that Jesus is the Christ, the Son of God; and that believing ye might have life through his name.***[110]

"James, you may still be thinking that your case is hopeless. But Jesus came to save you, not to condemn you. So the wedding is not for just a few. It's for all that put their faith in Jesus. After all, He died that you might be saved." In the Revelation of Jesus Christ we find that:

> ***After this I beheld, and, lo, <u>a great multitude, which no man could number</u>, of all nations, and kindreds, and people, and tongues, stood before the throne, and before the Lamb, clothed with white robes, and palms in their hands... And one of the elders answered, saying unto me, What are these which are arrayed in <u>white robes</u>? and whence came they? And I said unto him, Sir, thou knowest. And he said to me, These are <u>they which came out of great tribulation</u>, and <u>have washed their robes, and made them white in the blood of the Lamb</u>.***[111]

"So you see, there will be a great deliverance after the tribulation. And now we can unlock Samson's riddle of the garments."

> ***And the spirit of the LORD came upon him, and he went down to Ashkelon, and slew thirty men of them, and took their spoil, and gave <u>change of garments</u> unto them which <u>expounded the riddle</u>.***[112]

"You see, the change of garments was the explanation for the riddle." "So what does it mean to be given a change of garments?

---

110 John 20:31.
111 Revelation 7:9, 13, 14.
112 Judges 14:9.

I see the correlation between the riddles but how does this explain the riddle?"

Christ Gives You a New Garment

"The bigger question is, when you pass into eternity, will you place your destiny into the hands of Christ or Satan? Christ is pleading the cases of all who pass into eternity."

> *If we confess our sins, he is faithful and just to forgive us [our] sins, and to cleanse us from all unrighteousness.*[113]

"But Satan will also plead that you should be numbered with him as illustrated in the case of Joshua, the high priest. We will appear in judgment with filthy garments and fallen countenances. Yet Christ will over-rule Satan if we place our trust in Him for Jesus has the power to forgive our sins."[114]

> *And he showed me Joshua the high priest standing before the angel of the LORD [Jesus], and Satan standing at his right hand to resist him. And the LORD [Jesus] said unto Satan, The LORD rebuke thee, O Satan; even the LORD that hath chosen Jerusalem rebuke thee: [is] not this a brand plucked out of the fire? Now Joshua was clothed with filthy garments, and stood before the angel. And he answered and spake unto those that stood before him, saying, Take away the filthy garments from him. And unto him he said, Behold, I have caused thine iniquity to pass from thee, and I will clothe thee with change of raiment.*[115]

"Some day you and I will be standing in the judgment just like Joshua. And we too will be wearing the filthy rags of our sins."

---

113 1 John 1:9.
114 Luke 5:24.
115 Zechariah 3:1-4.

THE CHANGE OF GARMENT EXPLAINS THE RIDDLE: As Jesus explained to Nicodemus, we must be borne again and cast off our filthy robes of sin and put on robes of righteousness; the wedding garments of heaven.

You may recall that the Holy Spirit descended upon Jesus at His baptism as a robe from heaven. Likewise, Elijah gave his robe to Elisha. Study these events and you'll learn more about the Robe of Righteousness.

5 *Friend of the Bridegroom*

He that hath the bride is the bridegroom: but the <u>friend of the bridegroom</u>, which standeth and heareth him, rejoiceth greatly because of the bridegroom's voice: this my joy therefore is fulfilled. He must increase, but I [must] decrease.[116]

Best men have the responsibility of preparing the way for the wedding. The best man is involved in the preparation of the wedding, taking care of the bride, and making preparations for the groom. But before the wedding, the role of the Best Man must decrease and the role of the groom must increase.[117] John the Baptist was far more than a companion and cousin to Jesus. He recognized that he was *the friend of the bridegroom* and the *best man*. John is a role model for you and me. He preached the good news and was a voice in the wilderness of sin, preparing the way of the Lord. John proclaimed his role as Christ's Best Man:

> *He that hath the bride is the bridegroom: but the <u>friend of the bridegroom</u>, which standeth and heareth him, rejoiceth greatly because of the bridegroom's voice: this my joy therefore is fulfilled. He must increase, but I [must] decrease.*[118]

John's preaching spread far beyond the borders of Judea, even to Rome, preparing the Way of the Lord. John drew a large following and many thought that he was the Messiah. John's popularity soon rose above the rulers and priests of Israel who grew to despise him because he threatened their power.

---

116 John 3:29, 30.
117 John 3:30.
118 John 3:29, 30.

> *John did baptize in the wilderness, and preach the baptism of repentance for the remission of sins.*[119]

John is a type of Christ and his mission was prophesied by the prophet Malachi, his birth like that of Christ's was announced by the angel Gabriel, he was great in the sight of the Lord, he preached the good news, he baptized many, he had many disciples, and he died a martyr. Yet John consistently directed the attention of his followers to the one he referred to as the *Lamb of God.* Both John and Jesus would fulfill prophecy and therefore John must decrease as Jesus increased. Like Samson and Jesus, John was announced by an angel and he was to be a Nazarite from birth:

> *the angel said unto him, Fear not, Zacharias: for thy prayer is heard; and thy wife Elisabeth shall bear thee a son, and thou shalt call his name John. And thou shalt have joy and gladness; and many shall rejoice at his birth. For he shall be great in the sight of the Lord, and shall drink neither wine nor strong drink; and he shall be filled with the Holy Ghost, even from his mother's womb. And many of the children of Israel shall he turn to the Lord their God.*[120]

LINK 18: Bridegroom's Friend

Before I left New Orleans, I had one more meeting with James to show him the rest of the connections between Samson and Jesus. "John and Jesus were co-workers in establishing a new movement that promised the remission of sins. Rather than follow the practices of sacrificial offerings for sins, they practiced water baptism."

> *After these things came Jesus and his disciples into the land of Judaea; and there he tarried with them, and baptized. And John also was baptizing in Aenon near to*

---

119 Mark 1:3, 4.
120 Luke 1:13-16.

Salim, because there was much water there: and they came, and were baptized.[121]

"As a consequence of the revived approach, they drew many of their followers away from the priests and rabbis and had large followings." "Did John invent the practice?" "No. Water baptism wasn't some new fad that was invented by John and Jesus. The practice of water baptism had its early origins in the Old Testament, for example in the account of Naaman. Naaman was a leper and sought out Elisha, the prophet of God to heal him. Elisha directed Naaman to dunk himself seven times in the Jordan and after Naaman had followed Elisha's instructions his skin was as fair as a new born baby." "Why? Was there something special about the waters of the Jordan?" "No, because Naaman humbled himself before God; it pleased God to heal him. God knew that Naaman's heart was ready to be converted to follow Him."

And he returned to the man of God, he and all his company, and came, and stood before him: and he said, Behold, now I know that [there is] no God in all the earth, but in Israel.[122]

"John and Jesus were bound together in the same mission. Both led their disciples to baptize new believers. John was the Voice in the Wilderness that would usher in Jesus. Jesus would complete the mission." "Don, how does this tie to Samson?" "Well, Samson was the bridegroom and the Scriptures tell us that one of Samson's companions was the friend; that is, he was the *friend of the bridegroom.*"

Samson's wife was [given] to his companion, whom he had used as his friend.[123]

---

121 John 3:22, 23.
122 2 Kings 5:15.
123 Judges 14:20.

Event Sequence Analysis

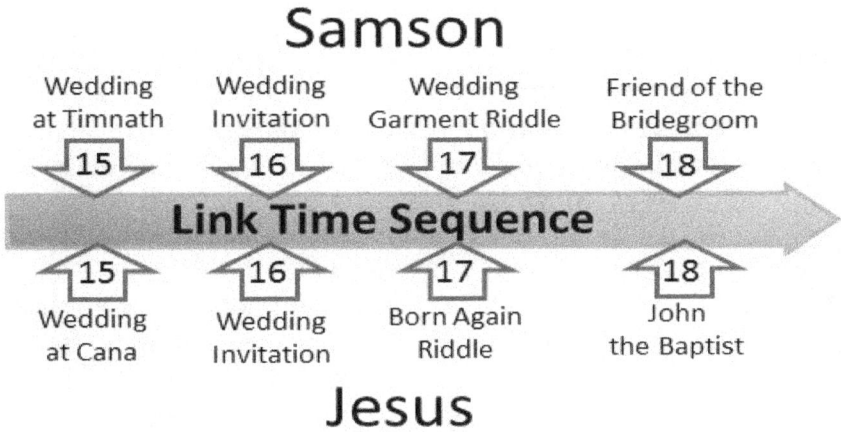

Samson

Wedding at Timnath	Wedding Invitation	Wedding Garment Riddle	Friend of the Bridegroom
15	16	17	18

Link Time Sequence →

15	16	17	18
Wedding at Cana	Wedding Invitation	Born Again Riddle	John the Baptist

Jesus

18 Links in a Row

The event-time sequence of similar parallel events and associations underscore the supernatural connection between Samson and Jesus. The likelihood of these 18 events occurring in both the lives of Samson and Jesus is nearly beyond comprehension. To put this in probabilistic terms it's like finding a single star in all the stars of the Universe or about 1 in 10^{29}.

D.H.ALEXANDER

6 *Fields Afire*

After these things the Lord appointed other seventy also, and sent them two and two before his face into every city and place, whither he himself would come. And the seventy returned again with joy, saying, Lord, even the devils are subject unto us through thy name.[124]

One lazy, hot summer July afternoon in Northeast Washington State, we found ourselves returning from a visit to Grandpa Virgil's farm northwest of Spokane. As we travelled through the rolling scablands that had been carved by the Missoula Flood we could see dust devils rising from the plowed fields along the highway. We could see the basalt lined canyons that were carved by the Ice Age waters. Immense volumes of water, estimated to be roughly equivalent to half of Lake Michigan, were released from the ice dam that broke near Missoula, Montana thousands of years ago. The flood waters were over 300 feet deep (roughly three times the height of the tsunami that hit Fukushima) as they raced at an estimated 65 miles per hour over the site of present day Palouse Falls. It was plenty sufficient to deepen the gorge between Washington and Oregon. I wondered how Creationists or atheists for that matter would explain this flood? For many decades geologist J. Harlen Bretz was ostracized for introducing a regional hypothesis for the reshaping of the Columbia Basin by a huge flood.[125] It wasn't until the 1950's that the hypothesis that Bretz proposed for the flood features of the Columbia Basin was widely accepted. Scientists now realize that a high wall of water tore through the basin. The scientific mindset is slow to change. But it's one thing to provide evidence of a regional flood and quite another to get science to embrace the worldwide Flood of Noah.

---

124 Luke 10:1, 17.
125 Bretz, J Harlen (1923). "The Channeled Scabland of the Columbia Plateau". Journal of Geology 31: 617–649.

By the end of summer the fields of Northeast Washington State are so dry that lightning storms can set the fields on fire. Most years we can periodically smell smoke drifting from forest fires to the west billowing across the hills accompanied by a dusty dull gray sky. But when range fires are ignited in a dry field the fire wall surges upwards of thirty feet high or more and is a frightening site even from miles away.

As we cruised south along the four-lane, we talked about how wonderful it would be to share our findings with others. After several years of study, I was convinced that the Scriptures provided the evidence of God. My wife happily agreed. She had gently and patiently encouraged me every step of the way, providing me with references and insights that she had picked up over the years. Suddenly, even as we talked about sharing our findings, the dreaded red engine light flashed and the engine temperature jumped as steam billowed out from under the hood of our car.

The odd thing is that we both rejoiced because we were convinced that God was answering our prayer. And little did we know it then, but He was about to provide us with a set of experiences that we would remember for the rest of our lives. He was giving us an opportunity to meet with people that needed to hear what we had to share. The Scriptures record numerous occasions when the Lord intervened in the lives of men to accomplish evangelism. Even in the life of Samson, it is written that:

> *his father and his mother knew not that it [was]* <u>*of the LORD, that he sought an occasion*</u> *against the Philistines: for at that time the Philistines had dominion over Israel*[126]

So it would be for us. The Lord had sought an occasion for us to share our message. Fortunately, our car began to overheat within about a mile of the only rest stop on that long stretch of freeway. Fortunately, you ask? Yes! Coincidence? No! We were still smiling as we brought our car safely to the curb. When the tow

---

126 Judges 14:4.

truck driver arrived, we had an important decision to make. He could take us to our home in Richland, Washington some 60 miles south or he could take us to a little country town that we had passed about 30 miles earlier. He assured us that there were hotel accommodations and an excellent dealership that could repair our Chrysler LHS in that small town at the intersection of two major freeways.

Even though we were travelling with our daughter and young son we decided to put our experience in God's hands. And besides we thought, how long could it take to repair the car; maybe a day or two at the most? It would force us to take a short, much needed vacation. I would call the office in the morning and explain our predicament. And so we rode with the truck driver we told him how happy we were that God had plans for us. He dropped us off at a little hotel within walking distance of the car dealership and within walking distance of all necessary conveniences. We settled in for the night like expectant children waiting for Christmas morning.

Divine Appointment

At the break of day we headed to a nearby store just off Main Avenue to buy food for breakfast. When we finished eating, our daughter Robyn begged us to take her to the library that fortunately was located just a short walk from our hotel. Robyn became so happily preoccupied with books that we decided to let her enjoy herself and we took our baby son for a stroll down Main Street.

It wasn't long before we came to a little shop appropriately called the Olive Branch. It was a warm sunny day and a gentleman wearing a kippah was sitting on a bench just outside the entrance. We asked if he was Jewish but he responded that he was Messianic. I said, "Oh so you're a Messianic Jew." But he responded emphatically, "**No! I'm Messianic.**"

It turned out that the Messianic that we'll call Harry owned the shop. Harry stood up, waved us in and showed us around. He explained that most of the artwork on display was painted or crafted by local artisans and the items were sold on commission. As we wandered through the shop I came upon several large shelves of Jewish literature along the back counter. I spotted several books that I knew would fill in information that I needed to help me unlock the secrets of the Sanctuary and I was anxious to purchase them.

I took several books from the shelves put them on the counter and I asked Harry how much he was asking for them since they didn't have a price tag. Harry replied, "They aren't for sale." Again, I countered, "How much are they? I need them." Again he replied, "They aren't for sale." The conversation repeated itself as our voices grew louder.

Finally, Harry looked at me with a curious smile and sighed, "Why do you need these books so urgently?" I replied, "I'm writing a book." He countered, "What's the book about?" So I started to tell him about what I had found in the account of Samson. But before I revealed the hidden message he waved his hand and said, "Wait! Could you come back at 3:00 PM? There are others that I would like you to share your discovery with." I said "Sure, we don't have anything else to do because our car broke down on the highway and it's being repaired down the street at the Chrysler dealership." So we went back to the hotel and settled the kids down wondering what God had in store for us.

Finally, the hour was near so JaNa and I headed back to the Olive Branch, just three blocks away. As we walked through the door to the shop we saw Harry talking to a man who was sitting in a large comfortable stuffed chair. The man was a tall strong farmer wearing overalls, a flannel shirt and suspenders, and a baseball cap. And there was a young blonde headed boy on his lap. Harry motioned me over and asked me to sit down next to the gentleman. He introduced me to Josef as I sat down. Without any further ado, Harry said, "Don, please tell Josef what you were telling me earlier."

As I began to unfold the miraculous revelation hidden in the shadows of the account of Samson, Josef was moved nearly to tears. So I stopped and asked Josef why he appeared to be so sad yet joyful. Josef replied, "You were sent by God for this moment." I was exceedingly surprised and replied, "Why do you say that?" And he responded, "Because we buried my son this past week. He was killed in a farming accident. God has sent you here."

With the excitement of the revelation of Samson upon his face, Josef invited us to his home after dinner so that we could tell his family what we had told him. Samson had convinced him that God lives. I replied, "I'm sorry Josef but our car's broken down and we have no way to get to your home." Immediately, Harry interceded and said, "I'll be glad to pick you up and take you to Josef's place."

So that evening, as we rode across the rolling hills it seemed like we could see nothing but blue sky for miles above endless fields of golden grain. It was a beautiful summer evening and we wondered what God had in store for us. After about twenty minutes we crested yet another hill and Harry pointed to the west near two grain elevators and he said, "There's the farm." As we entered the farm, we saw numerous homes surrounding a large facility that served as their community work center, kitchen, and dining hall. Numerous other farm buildings and shops were arranged along the driveway where they parked machinery and large trucks that they used to take potatoes to market. I loved the place right away because my wife and I both come from "country" backgrounds. I'd been raised on a tree farm in upstate New York and JaNa had been raised on a farm in Northeastern Washington.

As we pulled into the driveway we were met by Josef and a host of welcoming faces. Josef hurried us along because a large crowd had been invited to hear our discoveries and were all patiently waiting inside. As he opened the door and welcomed us in, I saw Josef's sisters and their children all politely sitting in a big circle with chairs set up in front.

As nearly as I could tell, there were nearly thirty people all told. The women wore long solid colored dresses trimmed in white with coverings on their heads. They reminded me of the Amish that I had frequently talked with as I drove through northeastern Pennsylvania. The Amish sold fruits and vegetables along road-side stands and were well known for their isolation from the modern world. As I walked through the door, I felt as if we had stepped across the threshold of a very spiritual place. I also knew that these people showed a reverence for God seldom seen in the outside world. They held regular weekly church services, held prayer meetings, and studied their Bibles. The families made me feel so welcome with their excited smiling faces that I felt like I was home. The parents all quietly and politely sat in the back of the room and the children sat up front where I was invited to sit. But at that moment, I felt unworthy. After all, who was I to talk to these people about the God they already loved? But looking back I now realize that God had arranged the appointment. Samson was the instrument that God had appointed.

Fox Tale

Josef immediately prompted me to tell his family members what I had told him earlier in the day. After some introductions I began to tell them what I had learned from my study of Samson. Samson was the perfect place to start because all the children knew about Samson. In fact, I soon learned that the children knew more about the accounts of Samson, David and Goliath, and Jonah than most adults. Children are galvanized by the superhero stories of the Bible. I now realize that God planned it that way.

As I looked at the young farm boys sitting up front, I asked, "Have you ever caught a fox?" They shook their heads no. So I asked, "Can you imagine capturing not five, not ten, not a hundred, but three hundred foxes?" They giggled shaking their heads as I asked the question. One blonde haired boy said, "Foxes are hard to catch. They're really fast and smart." I said, "It's hard to imagine that anyone could capture that many foxes. Samson caught those three hundred foxes alright but catching them was the easy part."

That got the children's attention. If that was easy…what did he do that was even harder?

I singled out a couple of the older, stronger looking boys and asked, "Do you boys think you could tie the tails of two foxes together?" They just laughed. One little girl laughed and said, "They'll bite you!" "You're right," I replied. Then I lowered my voice and quietly said, "So imagine what would happen if you had to tie one hundred and fifty pairs of foxes tails together!" They looked at me in disbelief. I heard someone say, "Yah right!"

The children sitting before me routinely studied their Bibles, so I knew that they were familiar with the account of Samson. So I asked, "What did Samson do with the foxes?" And one young Bible scholar said, "He let them go and they set the fields on fire." "Almost," I replied, "but he performed an important feat first!"

Firebrand

"Have any of you ever used a torch?" One of the older teenagers replied, "Some farmers 'round these parts used torches to burn the stubble off the fields." "Right!" I exclaimed. "In Samson's day they used torches to burn off their fields too.

Do you do any branding?" "Yah and we tag them." someone said referring to their cattle. So I continued, "Now is there anyone here that would tie a firebrand to the tails of a pair of foxes?" Again laughter filled the room. "Not just one pair but one hundred and fifty pairs of foxes. Well, after Samson tied the tails of two foxes together, he tied a firebrand to their tails. How do you think the foxes reacted?" One of the younger boys said, "They would have been fighting like wildcats to get away from the fire. Animals are afraid of fire." I nodded in agreement. "Well children, you know what happened next. Samson let the foxes go with their firebrands bouncing along behind them setting the Philistines fields afire!"

Meaning of Samson's Foxes

"What does this have to do with Jesus?" I asked. "What do the fields symbolize?" No one had an answer. So I repeated what I had told Josef earlier. "Jesus tells us that the "field" is a symbol of the World!"[127] So I made the bold statement, "Samson set the fields on fire and Jesus set the world on fire." "But how did Jesus set the world on fire?"

They all stared excitingly waiting for the punchline. So I said, "Samson set the field on fire by sending the foxes out two by two just as Jesus sent His disciples out two by two." And I opened my Bible and read to them from a passage of the Gospel of Mark:

> *And he called [unto him] the twelve, and began to send them forth by two and two; and gave them power over unclean spirits; And they went out, and preached that men should repent. And they cast out many devils, and anointed with oil many that were sick, and healed [them].[128]*

"Why did the author of the Scriptures use foxes?" And one of the boys replied, "Because they're wise." "Thank you!" I replied. "Jesus told the disciples and apostles to be careful as they travelled."

> *Behold, I send you forth as sheep in the midst of wolves: be ye therefore wise as serpents, and harmless as doves.[129]*

LINK 19: Foxes Two by Two

After the events of Jesus birth and childhood, he was driven into the wilderness to meet with Satan in a contest for the Kingdom. Through His Temptation, Jesus defeated Satan, the roaring lion,

---

127 Matthew 13:38.
128 Mark 6:7, 12, 13.
129 Matthew 10:16.

SENT OUT TWO BY TWO: Samson sends out the foxes two by two to set the field on fire just as Jesus sent the Disciples out two by two to set the world on fire. The first was by physical fire, the second was by the fire of the Holy Spirit.

SENT OUT TWO BY TWO: Jesus sent the disciples out two by two and they set the world on fire. Jesus said the field is the world. [Matthew 13:38].

just as Samson had been driven by the Spirit into the wilderness where he defeated another roaring lion. One defeated a supernatural lion, the other defeated a physical lion. As the account of Mark proceeds, John the Baptist is imprisoned and John and his followers are under persecution by the church leaders as was Jesus and His followers. And so, as it is written in the Gospel according to Mark, Jesus sends his disciples into the world two by two. ***And he called [unto him] the twelve, and began to send them forth by two and two; and gave them power over unclean spirits.***[130] Jesus sent them out two by two in spiritual warfare. Jesus would attack the enemy by sending His apostles out to battle against Satan's unclean spirits. Samson would send out the foxes two by two to set the Philistines fields on fire.

LINK 20: Firebrands

Samson tied firebrands to the tails of the foxes and the firebrands were set ablaze. Likewise, Jesus set the apostles on fire by filling them with the Holy Spirit. The first is physical fire; the second is supernatural fire.

LINK 21: Fields on Fire

In the parable Jesus says, ***the field is the world; the good seed are the children of the kingdom; but the tares are the children of the wicked [one]; The enemy that sowed them is the devil.***[131] Once again we see that Jesus uses an example of physical reality to explain the Supernatural War that is being waged with Satan. When Jesus sent the apostles out into the field (or world) they set the field on fire. They took the fire that was in them and lit other human candles around them. As each new person was ablaze with the Holy Spirit, the spirit's fire and glow spread like a wildfire. Not only were they healing the sick and freeing many from the grip of Satan's devils, but they were filling the people with the eternal

---

130 Mark 6:7.
131 Matthew 13:38, 39.

Hope of salvation. They began to realize that the work of John and Jesus was the way to free themselves from the sins of the world.

Mark Chapters 1 and 6

Perhaps you have your doubts about the sequence of events. I suggest you open your Bible and read Mark Chapters 1 and 6. And there you'll see the unfolding of events from the days of John the Baptist to the commissioning of the apostles. Just as Samson sent the foxes two by two with the firebrands tied to their tails to set the fields on fire, Jesus sent the apostles two by two into the world ablaze with the Holy Spirit to set the world on fire. Satan opposed the army of Christ by persecuting His followers. Since Satan couldn't tempt Jesus and cause Him to fall, he turned on those that Christ loved, like John the Baptist, to lure and trap Christ. John was a human casualty of that supernatural warfare. And Christ, increased His war on Satan by casting out demons.

Event Sequence Analysis

As you read through Mark Chapter 6, you'll prepare yourself to unlock the mystery of our next Chapter, Jawbone Hill.

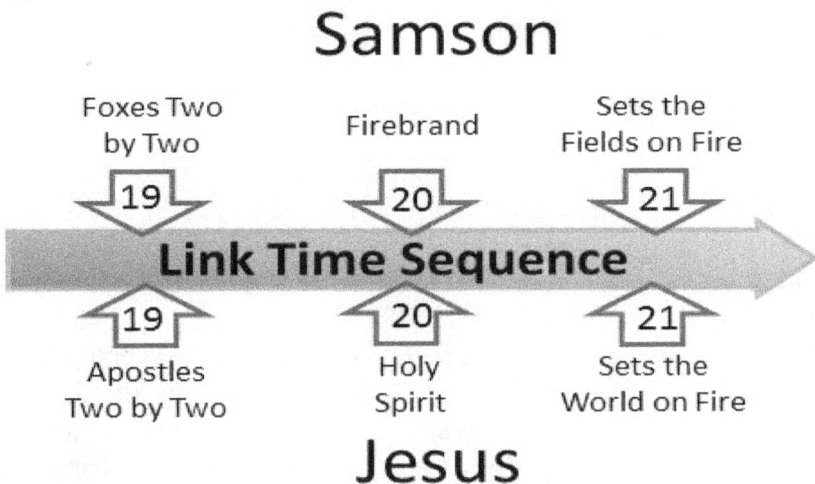

Samson

Foxes Two by Two	Firebrand	Sets the Fields on Fire
19	20	21

Link Time Sequence

19	20	21
Apostles Two by Two	Holy Spirit	Sets the World on Fire

Jesus

7 *Jawbone Hill*

And he smote them hip and thigh with a great slaughter: and he went down and dwelt in the top of the rock Etam [Judges 15:8].

The train picked up speed as it left the shores of Lake Pontchartrain and New Orleans faded from view. I was homeward bound on the train named the City of New Orleans heading north towards Chicago where I would make my transfer and head west. On this particular trip, I'd spent another week at Tulane University teaching another graduate course in the School of Tropical Medicine where I served for a number of years as a Clinical Professor. Over the course of those years, I was privileged with the opportunity to collaborate with James and co-chair the committees of three doctoral students with him. I benefitted because the research we conducted was associated with nuclear chemistry and health effects. It also gave me an opportunity to share my findings about Samson and test the reactions of other professors. To my pleasant surprise, the professors were very intrigued and have been asking for a copy of this book ever since. Their excited reactions encouraged and convinced me that open minded intellectuals and scientists would grasp the significance of the hidden patterns that I refer to as the Yeshua Code (Yeshua is the Hebrew name for Jesus, meaning to rescue or deliver).

By evening the skyline of Chicago came into view as we finally arrived at the Amtrak station. I soon boarded the Empire Builder which connects Chicago with Portland and Seattle. The train would drop me off along the route at my destination south of Spokane at Pasco, Washington. It was now evening and I was exhausted from my long days and late nights at the university and I was looking forward to a restful night's sleep on the Empire Builder. I was hoping to be rested enough that I would enjoy the approach to the Rocky Mountains and the awe inspiring leg through Glacier National Park.

Divine Appointment

I thought it would be a relaxing trip. But it was far more enjoyable than I could imagine. For it was on the return trip that God intervened with another Divine Appointment. Upon entering the Empire Builder at Chicago, I found my seat and secured my baggage and headed for the observation car to relax before I turned in for the night. As I arrived in the observation car the passengers were enjoying snacks served from the snack bar on the lower level and I soon recognized a young couple wearing Mennonite clothes. I soon struck up a conversation with them. I somehow began discussing my discovery of deeper patterns hidden within the Scriptures that had convinced me of the existence of God. But everyone was tired and we were soon headed back to our seats for the night. It was then that a gentleman by the name of John wearing denim jeans and a plaid flannel shirt politely tapped me on the shoulder and said that he'd overheard our conversation and was very interested in learning more. I suggested that we meet at 7:30 AM in the lower level snack bar so we could take enough time to do justice to the hidden messages that I'd found. He agreed and we both departed for our seats to catch some shut-eye.

I woke early and decided to take my laptop to the snack bar where there were several booths with electrical outlets. Fortunately, I found an empty booth and soon hooked up my computer so that I could review my findings. Shortly thereafter, my new found traveling companion came down the stairs and sat down across from me and we exchanged greetings and with John's prompting I began the conversation. "John, from a scientific view, the Old Testament is designed like an algebraic expression…that is, it's rich in symbols that often have multiple or at least dual meanings. For example, Jesus is referred to as the "***Lamb of God***." Although Jesus isn't literally a lamb, He's the worthy sacrifice that replaced the use of the lamb in the sacrificial system of the Old Testament."

After giving my companion a summary overview of my methods, research, and the patterns that I'd found, I launched into my findings on Samson. I opened by saying "John, I plan to show you that Samson is one of the best examples of Jesus that I've found in the Old Testament." John said. "Samson's not an obvious type of Christ to me. Why would you choose Samson when there are more obvious choices like Joseph, or David, or even Jonah?"

"To put it bluntly, the account of Samson is shocking. Within the account is hidden some of the strongest evidence for the existence of God." "Evidence of God?" He sounded surprised. "Yes, God! How could anyone accurately see events a thousand years into the future?" "The future?" "Some Being or Beings deliberately concealed the deeper meaning of future events within the life of Christ in Old Testament characters like Samson." "But how?" "Like a literary artist there are numerous key symbolic phrases in the account of Samson that tie him to Christ <u>all in order</u>." He looked both puzzled and surprised. So I showed him the following list:

- *Both Jesus and Samson were born at a time when Israel was under foreign rule,*
- *Both were miracle births,*
- *Their births were announced to their mothers by an angel,*
- *They would be miracle babies since Samson's mother was barren and Mary was a virgin,*
- *Both would be Deliverers of Israel,*
- *Their births were announced to their fathers by an angel,*
- *The angel referred to himself as "I AM" and Jesus claimed that "before Abraham was, I AM"*
- *Jesus is the Son of God and Samson's name means "Like the Sun,"*
- *Both would be moved by the Spirit to go forth and do battle with the enemy,*
- *Both were subjected to Temptation,*
- *Both sought the bride,*
- *Both defeat the roaring lion,*
- *Both begin their missions with a wedding (one at Timnath and the other at Cana),*
- *Both send them out two by two,*
- *Both set the fields, or should we say the world, on fire…*

After an hour of reviewing the details of the list John said, "It's clear that there's more to the account of Samson than the surface story." "Far more, I assure you." And then we reached a critical moment in our conversation. As a teacher, I like to sensationalize an important point so that it will be etched into the memories of my students and so I said, "***Samson killed thousands but Jesus has killed millions upon millions.***"

John looked astonished. And at that very moment, someone said "***how can you say such a thing?***" We realized that the slender middle-aged lady sitting in the booth behind us had been eavesdropping. "Come join us I urged. "No thank you but I'd like to listen."

The Word of God is designed to captivate our senses. It's designed to awaken us from our slumber. And it's mysteriously effective in reaching the heart. It's like a Physician's scalpel, ***sharper than any two-edged sword, piercing even to the dividing asunder of soul and spirit, and of the joints and marrow, and [is] a discerner of the thoughts and intents of the heart***"[132] The Sword of God had touched her heart and drew her into our conversation. She refused to sit with us in our small booth but she stood, listened, and hung onto every word. And then I explained...

LINK 22: Hip and Thigh

I said pointing to my hip, "Recall that Samson killed them ***hip and thigh***. Can you imagine anyone killing thousands of men by hitting them on their hips and thighs?" John replied, "That does seem a bit ridiculous doesn't it. Then what does the phrase ***hip and thigh*** mean?" "We'll have to go back to the account of Jacob wrestling with the Angel of the Lord to unlock the riddle. Recall that when the Angel of the Lord touched the hip and thigh of Jacob, he limped. John interjected "That's when Jesus, or should I say the Angel of the Lord changed the name of Jacob which means ***"Deceiver" to "Israel"*** which means ***overcomer***." "Right John!

---

132 Hebrews 4:12.

You see, Jacob was born again. **Jacob had overcome sin and was born again. He was an overcomer."** I pointed to the following verses:

> *Knowing this, that our old man is crucified with [him], that the body of sin might be destroyed, that henceforth we should not serve sin. For <u>he that is dead is freed</u> from sin.[133] Being born again, not of corruptible seed, but of incorruptible, <u>by the word of God,</u> which liveth and abideth forever.[134]*

"Recall the conversation between Jesus and Nicodemus. Jesus made it clear that we must be born again. You must die to self and be reborn as a new person in Jesus Christ. Putting it bluntly, symbolically you must be baptized." Then I pointed to the following verse: *Jesus answered and said unto him, Verily, verily, I say unto thee, Except a man be born again, he cannot see the kingdom of God.[135]* Again I said, **"Your old man must die and you must be born again."** So again I motioned to my jaw as I opened and closed it and then said, *"The hip symbolizes rebirth and the jawbone is a symbol of jawboning, speaking, and preaching.* The jawboning or should I say the preaching of Jesus led thousands to give their hearts to Him. As they listened to the power of the preaching of Jesus many died of their old-selves and were born again." Then both of my companions grinned ear to ear. "You see Jesus converted thousands on two main occasions in perfect parallel with the two jawbone slaughters of Samson. You'll recall that Jesus preached first to the five thousand and then to the four thousand."

> *Do ye not yet understand, neither remember the five loaves of the five thousand, and how many baskets ye took up? Neither the seven loaves of the four thousand, and how many baskets ye took up?[136]*

---

133 Romans 6:6, 7.
134 1 Peter 1:23.
135 John 3:3.
136 Matthew 16:9, 10.

"Likewise, Samson won the victory in two great slaughters involving thousands of Philistines shortly after Samson had set their fields on fire." I pointed John to the Scripture: *And he smote them **hip and thigh** with a great slaughter: and he went down and dwelt in the top of the rock Etam.*[137] "And in a second encounter the Scriptures show that Samson won against another group numbering a thousand."

[And] when he came unto Lehi, the Philistines shouted against him: and the spirit of the LORD came mightily upon him, and the cords that [were] upon his arms became as flax that was burnt with fire, and his bands loosed from off his hands. And he found a new jawbone of an ass, and put forth his hand, and took it, and slew a thousand men therewith.[138]

"You see John, Jesus converted many of His listeners on two key occasions through preaching. Metaphorically, He killed their sinful selves and they were reborn. Likewise, Samson killed men in two large battles by using the jawbone which symbolizes preaching." "I get it. What an amazing midrash." "Midrash?" "Jewish interpretation of difficult passages of the text... a kind of hermeneutics." Something told me that my companion John knew far more than I had given him credit for.

LINK 23: Jawboning

"John, preachers, like Billy Graham, are known to speak with great power. Graham held huge crusades and led thousands to Christ through baptism. You might say that he used God's two-edged sword to kill their old selves and they were transformed into a new way of life. And he did this *"heart surgery"* by jawboning or speaking. The size of the jawbone of an ass underscores the power of the spoken word. Jesus spoke to thousands from a mountain top and His voice carried for great distances like a mighty trumpet."

---

137 Judges 15:8.
138 Judges 15:14, 15.

Then John replied, "I think I'm beginning to understand. The **Power of His Word** is not that it's loud but that it transforms and or recreates millions of hearts." "I couldn't have said it better John." ***"The Power of Samson is the WORD of God."***

LINK 24: Great Slaughter

"Samson killed the Philistines in a *"**great slaughter**."* This connection between the use of the jawbone by Samson and the preaching power of Jesus also shows that Jesus was engaged in a battle against Satan." "So what you're saying professor is that Samson opposed the Philistines whereas Jesus opposed the forces of Satan that had taken the people captive." "Exactly John. Jesus set the captives free and converted thousands that had been ensnared by Satan including the demoniac and the demon possessed. Many misunderstood because they thought He had come to overthrow the Romans. But Jesus set the captives free from sin and death. Jesus was fulfilling His ministry just as He had proclaimed at the beginning of His ministry. Jesus came to set the captives free. He's still setting millions free through the Power of His Word."

LINK 25: Mountain Refuge

"John, I want you to note that in both cases Samson and Jesus sought a mountain refuge between their two battles. Jesus sought refuge from preaching and the spiritual battle. Samson sought refuge from the physical battle. Between the feeding of the 5000 and the 4000 Jesus went to the mountain to recharge." We found where the Scriptures say that **when he had sent the multitudes away, he went up into a mountain apart to pray: and when the evening was come, he was there alone** (Matthew 14:23). Likewise, Samson **smote them hip and thigh with a great slaughter: and he went down and dwelt in the top of the rock Etam** (Judges 15:8) which is just south of Bethlehem."

LINK 26: Kills Thousands

John was getting very excited. "This is an incredible riddle." "John, it's among my favorites. And here we see that following His rest in the mountain, Jesus fed the 4000. Likewise, after his rest in rock Etam, Samson killed a thousand a second time *hip and thigh* with the jawbone of an ass." "So the message is the conversion and death of the sinful man and the recreation of a saved being. Awesome...and all in the account of Samson!"

LINK 27: Ends Speaking

"Now John, I want you to notice what comes next. When Samson was finished with his slaughter the Scripture gives us substantiation of our interpretation of the jawbone as a symbol of preaching." John scanned the scripture and pointed to a key passage.

> *And it came to pass, <u>when he had made an end of speaking</u>, that he cast away the jawbone out of his hand...*[139]

"Wow professor that is incredible...it was all about speaking." "John, *the power of the Word of God is sufficient to recreate a new heart in us*. It has the power to convert us from our sinful nature." The Scriptures tell us that:

> <u>*By the word of the LORD were the heavens made*</u>*; and all the host of them by the breath of his mouth.*[140]

Ramathlehi: Jawbone Hill

Imagine the power of the words of Jesus. His voice had to carry with clarity over a great distance to reach ears of the 4000 and the

---

139 Judges 15:17.
140 PSALM 33:6.

5000. You may recall the voice heard from Mount Sinai when the Israelites arrived there after crossing the Red Sea. The voice of God sounded from the summit like a mighty trumpet (Exodus 19:19). It was on numerous occasions that Jesus preached upon the mount giving famous sermons, even the Sermon on the Mount (Matthew 5:1). It was on these occasions that the beauty of His sermons touched the hearts of the people and converted many." I pointed John again to where this is emphasized in the account of Samson. And Samson said,

With the jawbone of an ass, heaps upon heaps, with the jaw of an ass have I slain a thousand men. And it came to pass, when he had made an <u>end of speaking</u>, that he cast away the jawbone out of his hand, and called that place <u>Ramathlehi</u>[141]

"Many sinful hearts were destroyed by the beauty of His sermons as if by a powerfully compelling voice. And when he came to an end of speaking He cast away the jawbone. And He named the place Jawbone Hill." "Amazing."

Samson: Revelation of Jesus

"John, to put it bluntly, the account of Samson is shocking. Within the account is hidden some of the strongest evidence for the existence of God. But you need to translate the algebra to

> ***Strong's Lexicon 07437 Ramath Lechiy {raw'-math lekh'-ee}***
>
> Ramath-lehi = "height of a jawbone"

appreciate the beauty of the passages." "I would've never seen it." "John, superficially, the account of Samson[142] is a most unlikely example of the revelation of Jesus in the entirety of the Old Testament. Yet you shouldn't be surprised because Jesus tells us that the writings of the Old Testament are all about Him."

---

141 Judges 15:16, 17.
142 Hebrews 11:32 And what shall I more say? for the time would fail me to tell of Gedeon, and [of] Barak, and [of] Samson, and [of] Jephthae; [of] David also, and Samuel, and [of] the prophets...

"But the events in the account of Samson are outside our experiences. His life goes from one supernatural event to the next. Taken altogether it would be easy to conclude that the account of Samson is legend and lore that has grown beyond reality as it was passed from one generation to the next." "John, the Bible may appear, from a superficial perspective, to include Samson as the legend of a bigger than life character. But we're just beginning to align the links in the lives of Jesus and Samson. And it is shocking that at this juncture we've aligned 27 connections in the same order."

Event Sequence Analysis

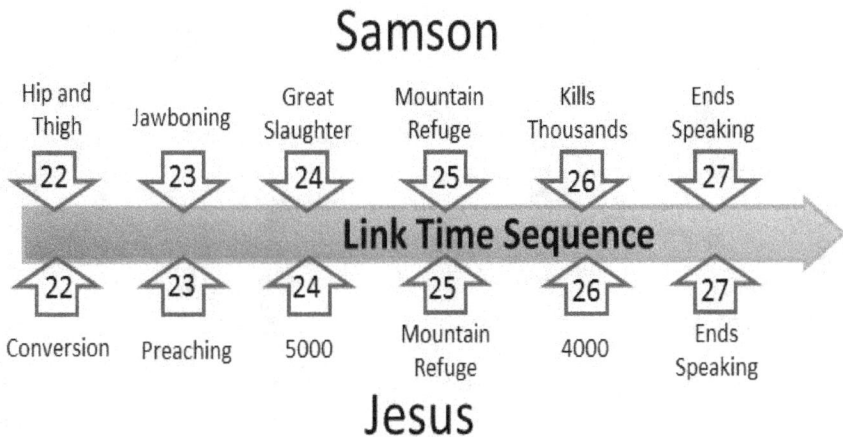

Samson

Hip and Thigh	Jawboning	Great Slaughter	Mountain Refuge	Kills Thousands	Ends Speaking
22	23	24	25	26	27

Link Time Sequence

22	23	24	25	26	27
Conversion	Preaching	5000	Mountain Refuge	4000	Ends Speaking

Jesus

27 Links in a Row

The event-time sequence of similar parallel events and associations underscore the supernatural connection between Samson and Jesus. The likelihood of these 27 events occurring in both the lives of Samson and Jesus is nearly beyond comprehension.

JESUS PREACHING TO THE 5000: For the word of God [is] quick, and powerful, and sharper than any two-edged sword, piercing even to the dividing asunder of soul and spirit [Hebrews 4:12]. The thousands that accepted Him as their savior died to their sins and were born again.

JAWBONING IS A SYMBOL OF PREACHING: As Samson killed thousands with the jawbone. Jesus converted thousands by jawboning or preaching. *The old man is a new creature: old things are passed away; behold all things are become new.* [2 Corinthians 5:17]. They are overcomers of sin.

8 Gates of Hell

I will build my church; and the gates of hell shall not prevail against it. [Matthew 16:18]

As the Empire Builder headed north through the Wisconsin Dells, my travelling companion's expression changed from one of mild amusement to the expression of sheer amazement. The look on his face reminded me of the look on the faces of my students when they reach an "aha" moment of sudden insight and understand how to balance a chemical equation for the first time. As a college professor, I've seen that look of discovery many times. But then curiously the expression on his face changed again.

John looked at me apologetically and said "I have a confession to make." I wondered what he meant by that as he continued, "I'm a pastor and I've never heard anyone open up the Scriptures as clearly as you have today. At first I didn't take you seriously but now I'm amazed at your deeper understanding of the Scriptures. After we get through our discussion of Samson could you please share your other findings?" His face was aglow, reminding me of the time when I first encountered these revelations and experienced a similar sense of euphoria. It made me wonder what it must have been like for those two men on the way to Emmaus.

There's joy that comes when you unlock the Scriptures. More profoundly, it provides the much sought-after evidence that God exists and His written WORD is a love letter. After all ***God is Love.*** I learned a long time ago that the Bible is no ordinary book. It has the power to transform lives, even the lives of professed students of the Scriptures. I said, "Sure pastor John, I'd be glad to. How long do we have?" He replied, "We have all day because I get off the train this evening at Whitefish." So we had at least 8 more hours to discuss my work and I had an educated audience.

I realized then, the importance of the revelations of the Scriptures that were being poured out upon us by the Holy Spirit. I also realized that even the very elect among us don't really have a grasp of the depth or the power of the Scriptures. I've seen similar reactions on the faces of many other pastors and scientists as I've shared the account of Samson. It never ceases to amaze me how powerful just 96 verses in the account of a single character like Samson can be so life-changing. I pray that you too will experience the transforming **Power of Samson**.

The Scriptures are like looking through a dark and distorted glass without seeing the account of Jesus and His Plan of Salvation woven behind the lives, events, systems, Feasts, and even objects.

> *When I was a child, I spake as a child, I understood as a child, I thought as a child: but when I became a man, I put away childish things. <u>For now we see through a glass, darkly; but then face to face:</u> now I know in part; but then shall I know even as also I am known. And now abideth faith, hope, charity, these three; but the greatest of these [is] charity.* "[143]

By studying the deeper message hidden behind these witnesses, we gain a more profound understanding of the Plan of Salvation than you can glean from the New Testament alone.

Unlocking the Scriptures

The pastor asked, "How do you unlock the Scriptures?" I replied, "This might sound trivial pastor, but the Scriptures provide their own keys. First you discover that most of the key words in the Scriptures have multiple meanings as you can learn by using Strong's Concordance to get to the context in the Hebrew or Greek usage. But the real secret is that the **timeline** in the Gospels provides the pattern and timeline for unlocking the Old Testament accounts." The pastor replied, "I use Strong's all the time."

---

143 1 Corinthians 13: 11-13.

"Pastor, I think of it this way. It's as if **the Old Testament is about Jesus and His Plan of Salvation concealed and the New Testament is about Jesus and His Plan of Salvation revealed**. Now that I look back over the years, I see a long line of witnesses that testify of Jesus Christ hidden within the verses of the Scriptures." I continued, "If we scan the Scriptures we find that the name Samson appears in only two books in the Bible: Oddly enough, in the account in the book of Judges and in the Book of Hebrews. In the Book of Hebrews, Samson is included among the great cloud of witnesses for Jesus Christ." Then I asked, "I wouldn't have considered Samson as a witness for Christ, would you?" He shook his head slowly and said, "Why no, I wouldn't." For emphasis I had him read the passage in Hebrews that says,

> *"Wherefore seeing we also are compassed about with so great a cloud of witnesses, let us lay aside every weight, and the sin which doth so easily beset [us], and let us run with patience the race that is set before us, Looking unto Jesus the author and finisher of [our] faith; who for the joy that was set before him endured the cross, despising the shame, and is set down at the right hand of the throne of God. And what shall I more say? for the time would fail me to tell of Gedeon, and [of] Barak, and [of] <u>Samson</u>, and [of] Jephthae; [of] David also, and Samuel, and [of] the prophets."*[144]

Importance of the Holy Spirit

So I said, "Why don't we unlock the next passage of the account of Samson together?" After Jawbone Hill (Ramathlehi) Samson was sore athirst:

> *and called on the LORD, and said, Thou hast given this great deliverance into the hand of thy servant: and now shall I die for thirst, and fall into the hand of the uncircumcised? But God <u>clave an hollow place that [was]</u>*

---

144 Hebrews 12:1, 2; Hebrews 11:32.

__in the jaw__, and __there came water thereout__; and when he had drunk, __his spirit came again__, and he revived: wherefore he called the name thereof Enhakkore, which [is] in Lehi unto this day.[145]

I said, "I hope you heard that." "He was revived by the Spirit!" "You're right pastor. According to Strong's Concordance *Enhakkore* means "*Spring of One Calling.*" In a parallel place in the sequence of the life of Jesus, the Scriptures say,

In the last day, that great [day] of the feast, Jesus stood and cried, saying, If any man thirst, let him come unto me, and drink. __He that believeth on me, as the scripture hath said, out of his belly shall flow rivers of living water. (But this spake he of the Spirit, which they that believe on him should receive__: for the Holy Ghost was not yet [given]; because that Jesus was not yet glorified."[146]

So I said, "Samson's Spring of One Calling is the parallel to the calling of Jesus. If we would just believe, the Holy Ghost would pour out of us just like it did from Jesus. You might note that, the spring flows out of the **JAW**. The Holy Spirit was flowing out from the mouth or **jaw(bone)** of Jesus to those that listened as He spoke. Of Samson the text speaks of physical water whereas in the parallel case of Christ the text speaks of spiritual water." "So Jesus is the Spring of One Calling. Awesome."

"Pastor, from the time of His Baptism, Jesus was filled with the Holy Spirit, and through prayer He was strengthened in His mission to free mankind from sin." Even upon the Cross,

Jesus knowing that all things were now accomplished, that the scripture might be fulfilled, saith, I thirst.[147]

---

145 Judges 15:18-19.
146 John 7:37-39.
147 John 19:28.

"Since the days of the apostles when the Holy Spirit was poured out at Pentecost, men have been given access to the same Comforter that strengthened Jesus." "That's what I preach."

LINK 28: Plots to Kill Them

"Pastor, after Jesus ministered to the 5000 and the 4000, supernatural warfare was ramped up to a new level. Both Samson and Jesus were rapidly moving to a deadly end. The Pharisees were plotting to kill Jesus, just as the Philistines were plotting to kill Samson. Satan had lost many of his captives because Jesus set the captives free through His sermons. So Satan stirred up his fallen followers to make war on Christ and His followers."

The pastor looked on anxiously and asked, "Well, what comes next?" So we turned to Judges 16, the last chapter that records the account of Samson in the Book of Judges:

> *Then went Samson to Gaza, and saw there an harlot, and went in unto her. [And it was told] the Gazites, saying, Samson is come hither. And they compassed [him] in, and laid wait for him all night in the gate of the city, and were quiet all the night, saying, In the morning, when it is day, we shall kill him. And Samson lay till midnight, and arose at midnight, and took the <u>doors of the gate of the city, and the two posts</u>, and went away with them, bar and all, and put [them] upon his shoulders, and carried them up to the top of an hill that [is] before Hebron.[148]*

Numerous places in the Scriptures tell us that time and time again, the Scribes and Pharisees sought to trap Jesus and kill Him.

> *After these things, Jesus walked in Galilee; for He would not walk in Jewry, because the Jews sought to kill Him.[149]*

---

[148] Judges 16:1-3.
[149] John 7:1.

LINK 29: Gates of Hell

Then I said, "Look forward in the chapter. Do you see another event in Judges 16 that reminds you of an event in the life of Christ?" Within seconds he said excitedly, "Why yes, Samson was sold for silver just as Jesus was!" In response I asked "What event took place between the feeding of the 5000 and the 4000 and the sale of Jesus for a few pieces of silver? What happened to Jesus that involved gates?" He looked unsure and he shook his head with a questioning look. So I replied, "Let's look in the account of Matthew." And there the pastor found the following passage:

> **<u>the gates of hell shall not prevail against it</u>. From that time forth began Jesus to show unto his disciples, how that he must go unto Jerusalem, and suffer many things of the elders and chief priests and scribes, and be killed, and <u>be raised again the third day</u>.**[150]

A big smile crossed the pastor's face and he asked "so are you saying that when Samson carried the gate to the top of the hill it parallels the account of Jesus carrying the Cross to Calvary?" "I am. And He metaphorically began to carry the door to the grave with Him also. Don't you agree?" That amazed look came across the pastor's face again as he replied. "Why yes...I do!"

---

150 Matthew 16:18, 21.

THE GATES OF HELL: Samson carried the gates that closed him in to the top of the Hill to escape death. Jesus carried the gates of the grave to Calvary to make us a way of escape from sin, eternal death, and the grave.

"Jesus had been bearing that Cross or should I say our burdensome sins for a long time. In the parallel, Samson was also carrying a gate; the Gate of the City. Plainly speaking Jesus was carrying the Gates of the graves to set the captives free. And Jesus took both the door and the two posts."

"Is the text suggesting that the two posts that He took with the door are sin and death?"

"Pastor John, it's as you suggest. Jesus was making a Way for us to escape sin and death."

LINK 30: Gate is the Door to the Grave

"So what is meant by the Gates of Hell?" I asked. The pastor said immediately, "you mean the prison gate to the grave?" And so I nodded in agreement and said, "yes, but it also means more. For sure, Jesus had them roll away the grave stone or gate to the tomb of His friend Lazarus. In that instance, Jesus had them roll away the stone to the tomb and then He called Lazarus from the realm of the dead and restored his life. Jesus proved in that moment that He has the power over death and the grave. But importantly, for you and me, when Jesus began His grand procession through the Sheep Gate during His Triumphal entry into Jerusalem, He was figuratively carrying the door to the tomb to the top of the hill on Calvary. That is, humanity would forever more have a way of escape from the grave and death."

LINK 31: Hill Far Away

"What Hill are we talking about professor?" "There were three primary hills in contention, the Mount of Olives, the Temple Mount, and Calvary. All of Christ's steps were leading to Calvary from the Mount of Olives to the Temple Mount and finally to Calvary. And if you like, to keep in accordance with our method,

Jesus went through the Sheep Gate on his way to the Temple. And this was very fitting since Jesus was the Lamb of God that taketh away the sins of the world. And we both know He ended His walk on Calvary as our sacrificial Lamb."

Event Sequence Analysis

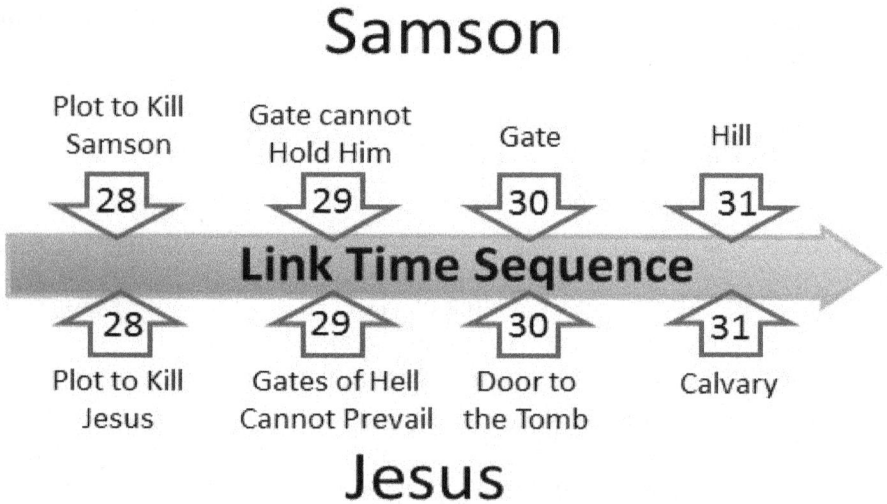

Samson

Plot to Kill Samson	Gate cannot Hold Him	Gate	Hill
28	29	30	31

Link Time Sequence

28	29	30	31
Plot to Kill Jesus	Gates of Hell Cannot Prevail	Door to the Tomb	Calvary

Jesus

Probability of 31 Links in a Row

We have now arrived at 31 links in the accounts of Samson and Jesus that occur in the same order. The odds of encountering 31 events in a row in two lives separated by more than a thousand years are on the order of 1 in 1×10^{54}.

9 *Who is Delilah?*

How is the faithful <u>city become an harlot</u>! it was full of judgment; righteousness lodged in it; but now murderers. Thy silver is become dross, thy wine mixed with water. [Isaiah 1:21,

In Bible prophecy a woman is a system of followers of either Christ or Satan. And we had come to the point in the account of Christ and Samson where a woman would play a main role. "Professor if all these events point to the life of Christ, then who's Delilah? Is she a symbol of Judas? After all she helped the Philistines trap Samson just as Judas met with the Pharisees to trap Jesus. And in both cases they sold them out for silver. I'd always wondered about the connection."

"You're on the right track but there's far more to the relationship than meets the eye," I replied. He tilted his head inquisitively and said, "Please explain." "We need to look at the spiritual context."

"Delilah and Judas are connected: she represents the traitorous Church and he represents the traitor that served the church. Delilah, like Judas, was being used as Satan's agent and weapon to sell out Samson, the proclaimed deliverer of Israel. Satan wanted to destroy Samson because he thought Samson was key to God's plan to rescue mankind. So Satan used Delilah as a pawn in the war with Christ." "A pawn?" "We're talking about the spiritual metaphor. Just as Samson risked his life for the woman, so too, Jesus was willing to lay down His life for the Church. Remember, a woman in Bible prophecy is not a single individual but she's the figure or symbol for the body of believers that we refer to as His Church."

"The literal bridegroom, did it out of lust of the flesh but Jesus did it out of genuine LOVE for the church. It grieved Jesus to see His church undergo persecution and He was willing to lay down His life so that the Church would live. And the deeper spiritual meaning is that Jesus would lay His life down for anyone who would believe in Him just as the shepherd will lay down his life in defense of his flock." I pointed to the following verse:

> *...even so must the Son of man be lifted up: That whosoever believeth in him should not perish, but have eternal life. For God so loved the world, that he gave his only begotten Son, that whosoever believeth in him should not perish, but have everlasting life. For God sent not his Son into the world to condemn the world; but that the world through him might be saved,[151]*

"So you see, Delilah is a symbol of the Church. It was Delilah that was used by Satan to trap Samson." The pastor replied, "So it was the church that was used by Satan as the temptress to trap Christ." "Yes pastor. After Satan lost the supernatural battle with Christ in the wilderness, the warfare for our souls began in earnest. Satan was more determined than ever to bring down Jesus. You could say that Satan pulled out all of the stops. He began using guerilla warfare tactics." "What do you mean by that?"

"You could say that Satan began to go around like a *roaring lion*. Christ had focused on saving the house of Israel but Satan caused many of the leaders to become like a brood of vipers.[152] They had long followed the subtle suggestions of Satan. Through Satan's corruption, the Jewish leaders became pawns in the supernatural battles. Even Peter was used as an avenue to tempt Jesus. Satan entered Peter and spoke through him in an attempt to change the course of Christ's mission. Satan spoke through Peter to dissuade Jesus from going to the Cross saying, *this shall not be unto thee*. But the all-knowing Christ discerned that it was Satan that had entered Peter. So Christ replied to Satan saying, *Get thee behind me Satan*."

Then Peter took him, and began to rebuke him, saying,

---

151 John 3:15-17.
152 Matthew 3:7.

Be it far from thee, Lord: <u>this shall not be unto thee</u>. But <u>he turned, and said unto Peter, Get thee behind me, Satan</u>: thou art an offence unto me: for thou savourest not the things that be of God, but those that be of men.[153]

"Pastor, the Scriptures tell us that we're the body of Christ." The pastor replied, "And if you're a part of the body of Christ you're a member of His Church. Satan used the church like a harlot."

Know ye not that your bodies are the members of Christ? shall I then take the members of Christ, and make [them] the members of an harlot? God forbid. What? know ye not that he which is joined to an harlot is one body? for two, saith he, shall be one flesh. But he that is joined unto the Lord is one spirit.[154]

"You need only look at the Scriptures to see the weapons in Satan's arsenal. You must admit that Satan is a dirty fighter because he resorts to unethical means. He tries to tempt and ensnare you and I unawares."

And take heed to yourselves, lest at any time your hearts be overcharged with surfeiting, and drunkenness, and cares of this life, and [so] that day come upon you unawares. For as a snare shall it come on all them that dwell on the face of the whole earth.[155]

"But he uses specific weapons in particular to tempt mankind and undermine Christ; the same three that he used against Samson. And he uses them to break up families." "Weapons? What weapons?"

---

153 Matthew 16:22, 23.
154 1 Corinthians 6:15-17.
155 Luke 21:34, 35.

Weapon One: Temptation by the Woman

"Satan uses an endless array of weapons and snares. But Samson's account brings out three of the most powerful supernatural weapons known to mankind."

"What do you mean by a supernatural weapon?" "Satan's supernatural weapons are temptations of the flesh that cause you to sin. And sin is a deadly wound. The Scriptures tell us that the wages of sin are death. Putting it another way, if we're tempted and fall to sin we'll ultimately die from our sin. And the death that I'm speaking of is not our mortal death but rather our spiritual death which is death eternal. Only Jesus, and Jesus alone, can rescue us from our sins. If Satan had caused Christ to fail, the kingdom would have fallen. In the wilderness, Christ was tempted three times but Christ avoided the bullets of temptation by defending Himself by quoting the Word of God."

"If Satan couldn't defeat Jesus in the wilderness then why did the warfare continue?" "Satan began to attack those that Christ loved. Satan hoped that he could cause Jesus to fall while Jesus was attempting to rescue those that He loves. And in the end, that's just what happened. But not the way Satan expected. Jesus allowed events to unfold so that the Plan of Salvation would be fulfilled. You might say that Jesus began to turn the tables on Satan on the way to the Cross."

"Satan uses the lusts of the flesh as a powerful weapon against those that love Christ. In simplistic terms, one weapon used by Satan is a man's lust after a woman. For example, David lusted after Bathsheba. Similarly, Samson lusted after Delilah and his lust led to his downfall. In David's case, he tried to cover his sins by murdering Uriah."

"The Scriptures provide a hint that Samson loved Delilah as a metaphor for Christ's love for the Church. In the end, both would be willing to die for the woman."

"The Scriptures say that, "it came to pass afterward, that he loved a woman in the valley of Sorek, whose name [was] Delilah."[156]

"You see the deeper meanings of the names are keys to unlock the deeper meaning of the Scriptures. Both Jesus and Samson were **_enfeebled_** or weakened by the woman. They both became broken-hearted and were so weakened by their grief that both were willing to die for them. When Jesus came to the Mount of Olives and looked over the splendor of Jerusalem, *"**He beheld the city, and wept over it.**"*[157] Jesus didn't grieve over His own impending death. He grieved over what might have been for Jerusalem. Because of their pride, scorn, and rejection of Him, He saw that they'd be doomed and their glory would be passed to the Gentiles. To Jesus, His flock was sweeter than the finest wine from the choicest vines."

> ### *Strong's Lexicon* 07796 Sowreq {so-rake'}
>
> Sorek = "choice vines" 1) a wadi in Palestine in which Delilah lived.
>
> 01807 Deliylah {del-ee-law'}
>
> Delilah = "feeble" 1) the Philistine mistress of Samson who betrayed the secret of his great strength, and by cutting his hair, enfeebled him and delivered him to the Philistines

The sceptre shall not depart from Judah, nor a lawgiver from between his feet, until Shiloh come; and unto him [shall] the gathering of the people [be]. Binding his foal unto the vine, and his ass's colt unto the choice vine; he

---

156 Judges 16:4.
157 Luke 19:41.

washed his garments in wine, and his clothes in the blood of grapes.[158]

"And so the Valley of Sorek represents the choicest of all humanity, even you and me if we make the right choice. And Jesus would come as the King upon the ass's colt to shed the blood of the winepress of "Sorek" for the woman, His Church.""

"Delilah's a symbol of those that were plotting against Samson; and in the parallel account those that would trap Jesus. Remember in our discussion of Samson's marriage, we talked about the two women?" The pastor nodded.

So I continued, "the pure woman represents the bride of Christ and Babylon the Great represents the bride of Satan. These two women symbolize all the human forces, individuals, and agencies that take the two sides in the supernatural conflict between Christ and Satan. One represents the army of the Lord and the other represents Satan's army. From another perspective, the two women represent the church of Christ and the church of Satan. And Delilah, like Judas, fell into Satan's trap."

"In the account of Samson, it's Delilah that collaborated with the Philistines to set traps that led to the capture of Samson. In the case of Jesus, Judas collaborated with the Pharisees to trap Him. In both cases Delilah and Judas are puppets acting under the influence of Satan. You see, Delilah represents the forces of Satan that were working through multiple avenues to bring down Jesus."

LINK 32: Satan's Church

"Pastor, it's clear that God allowed the acts of Delilah and Judas. And Satan took advantage of the opportunity believing that he had found a way to defeat Jesus."

The pastor scanned the scriptural account and replied, "So the Philistine leaders plotted to kill Samson, just like the Pharisees

---

158 Genesis 49:10,11.

plotted to kill Jesus, and both Judas and Delilah sold them out for silver, correct?" "Yes," I replied, "the Jewish leaders plotted to kill Jesus early on in Christ's ministry." I pointed to the place where Jesus read from the scroll of Isaiah at the beginning of His ministry:

> *The Spirit of the Lord [is] upon me, because he hath anointed me to preach the gospel to the poor; he hath sent me to heal the brokenhearted, to preach deliverance to the captives, and recovering of sight to the blind, to set at liberty them that are bruised, to preach the acceptable year of the Lord. And he closed the book, and he gave [it] again to the minister, and sat down. And the eyes of all them that were in the synagogue were fastened on him.*[159]

"The people that Jesus and His parents had worshipped with for three decades couldn't believe what they were hearing nor could they believe the confidence with which Jesus spoke. Imagine what must have been going through their minds. They must have questioned whether He was delusional. After all, with the passage of Isaiah He claimed to be the Messiah."

As I looked at the pastor I said, "Can you imagine the reaction of those in the synagogue that day? What if it happened in your church? What if one of the young adult members of your church walked to your pulpit, read a verse and claimed that he or she was the fulfillment of those verses? What if they claimed to be the Messiah? In no way did they believe that Jesus was the Messiah. After all he was an uneducated man raised in a carpenter shop in Nazareth." "You're right. We wouldn't allow it either." "Yet there He stood in front of all the people in full confidence that He was the Messiah. They were so angered that they set out to kill Him." And I said, "Look at the reaction of those in the synagogue that very day."

> *And all they in the synagogue, when they heard these things, were filled with wrath, And rose up, and thrust*

---

159 Luke 4:17-30.

him out of the city, and led him unto the brow of the hill whereon their city was built, that they might cast him down headlong. But he passing through the midst of them went his way.[160]

"Note that **all** they in the synagogue, not just a few, but **all** were filled with wrath. Based on the Scriptures, it was Satan that brought about their wrath. It was Satan, time and time again, that tried to stop the mission of the Savior. At every turn from His birth to His death, Satan sought every means possible to trip up Jesus and to cut short His mission. And he did this by turning those that Jesus loved against Him." In Luke and John we find:

the chief priests and scribes sought how they might kill him; for they feared the people. <u>Then entered Satan into Judas</u> surnamed Iscariot, being of the number of the twelve.[161]

and supper being ended, <u>the devil having now put into the heart of Judas Iscariot, Simon's [son], to betray him.</u>[162] *<u>And after the sop Satan entered into him.</u> Then said Jesus unto him, That thou doest, do quickly.*[163]

"Pastor, on a supernatural level there was a continuous war between Christ and Satan. And that war continues to this very day. But Satan realizes that he's defeated and it's just a matter of time until he is sentenced to eternal death. In the Book of Revelation it says:

Woe to the inhabiters of the earth and of the sea! for the devil is come down unto you, having great wrath, because he knoweth that he hath but a short time.[164]

---

160 Luke 4:28-30.
161 Luke 22:2, 3.
162 John 13:2.
163 John 13:27.
164 Revelation 12:12.

In the Old Testament it is written:

> ***And Satan stood up against Israel, and provoked David to number Israel.***[165]

> ***And the LORD said unto Satan, The LORD rebuke thee, O Satan; even the LORD that hath chosen Jerusalem rebuke thee: [is] not this a brand plucked out of the fire?***[166]

In the New Testament the war continued. "It was Satan that entered into Peter to tempt Jesus." The Scriptures say,

> ***But he turned, and said unto Peter, Get thee behind me, Satan: thou art an offence unto me: for thou savourest not the things that be of God, but those that be of men.***[167]

"Throughout the Scriptures the warfare between Christ and Satan continued since the war in heaven and it will continue until Satan is finally destroyed in the burning lake of fire." It is written:

> ***and the devil that deceived them was cast into the lake of fire and brimstone, where the beast and the false prophet [are], and shall be tormented day and night for ever and ever.***[168]

LINK 33: Philistines-Pharisees

"Pastor, when Samson sent the foxes into the fields two by two, the foxes set the fields on fire. When Jesus sent the apostles and disciples two by two, it was a supernatural assault on the armies of Satan. The apostles and disciples cast out demons and drove them away from the sheep of Israel. Satan's fallen angels were driven away by the Spirit of Christ.

---

165 1 Chronicles 21:1.
166 Zechariah 3:2.
167 Matthew 16:23.
168 Revelation 20:10.

And he called [unto him] the twelve, and began to send them forth by two and two; and gave them power over unclean spirits; And commanded them that they should take nothing for [their] journey, save a staff only; no scrip, no bread, no money... And they went out, and preached that men should repent. And they cast out many devils, and anointed with oil many that were sick, and healed [them].[169]

"Similarly, the Philistines were angered that their fields were set on fire just as the Pharisees were angered when the Apostles, in a spiritual context, set their world on fire. You could say that it was a blow to the livelihood of both. The blow to the Philistines was not just a blow to their ego. It impacted them economically." "They must have been very angry." "They were, but behind it all, it was Satan that was angered. His forces were being defeated by the Apostles and disciples. The Apostles and disciples were driving Satan's forces out of, and away from, those that they had possessed."

She Tried to Ensnare Him

"Delilah tried to ensnare Samson on three separate occasions before she finally turned him over to the Philistines." I pointed to the three passages in Chapter 16 of the Book of Judges where the *lords of the Philistines* tried to ensnare Samson:

- bound *with seven green withs that were never dried, then shall I be weak, and be as another man* (Judges 16:7);
- bound *with new ropes that never were occupied, then shall I be weak, and be as another man* (Judges 16:11);
- she wove the *seven locks of my head with the web* (Judges 16:13).

---

169 Mark 6:7-13.

"Pastor, none of these attempts worked. Likewise, the lords of the church tried multiple times to ensnare Jesus before Judas turned Him over to the Pharisees. None of these attempts worked either."

- *And rose up, and thrust him out of the city, and led him unto the brow of the hill whereon their city was built, that they might cast him down headlong* (Luke 4:29, 30);
- Jesus healed the sick on the Sabbath. And looking round about upon them all, he said unto the man, Stretch forth thy hand. *And he did so: and his hand was restored whole as the other. And they were filled with madness; and communed one with another what they might do to Jesus* (Luke 6:7-11).
- Jesus cleansed the temple at the beginning and end of his ministry. And he said unto them, *Is it not written, My house shall be called of all nations the house of prayer? but ye have made it a den of thieves. And the scribes and chief priests heard [it], and sought how they might destroy him: for they feared him, because all the people was astonished at his doctrine* (Mark 11:15-18).

"Neither Jesus nor Samson could be taken captive by their captors until the appointed time had arrived." "So it was all worked out ahead of time...step by step." "You might better say that all was seen ahead of time." "I get your point professor." "Jesus could have avoided capture as He had many times in the past. He could pass right through them if it pleased Him. But the time had arrived. Likewise, Samson finally relented and let the woman, or should we say the symbol of the church, capture him. Both were following their paths of intertwined destinies."

10 *Sold Out for Silver*

For the love of money is the root of all evil: which while some coveted after, they have erred from the faith, and pierced themselves through with many sorrows. [1Timothy 6:10].

Money is the root of all evil. The pastor asked, "If the first weapon is the lust of the flesh or *"for the love of a woman,"* what's the second? My guess is that Satan uses money as the second weapon because money is the root of all evil!" Again I replied, "Yes but not exactly. On one level you're right. But like the first weapon the second weapon also has a deeper meaning. It's far more than money. You might say that money is a medium of exchange?"

"Are you suggesting that money's a satanic medium?"

"Yes! It's like an intervening medium or means through which satanic agencies can enter us and impress us. It's like an addictive drug or alcohol. They all provide a door to our minds through which Satan can enter. I'm not saying that money's all bad. Jesus wouldn't have used money at all in His ministry if it was bad in and of itself. Depending on the condition of our hearts, money can be used for good or evil. It's a medium or channel for temptation. It's the lust of the eyes." Then the pastor quoted the Scriptures:

> *for the love of money is the root of all evil: which while <u>some coveted after</u>, they have erred from the faith, and pierced themselves through with many sorrows.*[170]

---

170 1 Timothy 1:10.

"Notice that the verse says while some coveted after... Covet is the key word. Whatever a man covets in this world can be used by Satan as a snare. It could be "love" or lust of the flesh, power, riches, pleasures, objects; it could be any of a number of things that divert our attention from God." Jesus warns us to:

take heed to yourselves, lest at any time your hearts be overcharged with surfeiting, and drunkenness, and cares of this life, and [so] that day come upon you unawares. For as a snare shall it come on all them

> **1 John 2:15 Love not the world, neither the things [that are] in the world. If any man love the world, the love of the Father is not in him. 2:16 For all that [is] in the world, the lust of the flesh, and the lust of the eyes, and the pride of life, is not of the Father, but is of the world. 2:17 And the world passeth away, and the lust thereof: but he that doeth the will of God abideth for ever.**

that dwell on the face of the whole earth. Watch ye therefore, and pray always, that ye may be accounted worthy to escape all these things that shall come to pass, and to stand before the Son of man.[171]

"The Scriptures also tell us, *Love not the world, neither the things that are in the world. If any man love the world, the love of the Father is not in him. For all that is in the world, the lust of the flesh, and the lust of the eyes, and the pride of life, is not of the Father, but is of the world.*"[172]

"So what does this have to do with Judas and Delilah?"

---

171 Luke 21:34-36.
172 1 John 2:15, 16.

Medium of Exchange

"Everyone knows that Judas sold Jesus out for silver but is there more?"

"Much more" I assured. "We need to look behind the motives of Judas to get a better appreciation for why he sold out Jesus. And we'll find that we're in some ways guilty of the same sins!"

"You'll recall that Judas acted as the treasurer for the ministry of Christ and His apostles. And judging by the Scriptures he was very tight with funds." "Yes, he contested the oil that was to be used by Mary to anoint Jesus." And the pastor found the place in the Scriptures where it said:

1 Timothy 6:9 But they that will be rich fall into temptation and a snare, and [into] many foolish and hurtful lusts, which drown men in destruction and perdition.

6:10 For the love of money is the root of all evil: which while some coveted after, they have erred from the faith, and pierced themselves through with many sorrows.

Then saith one of his disciples, Judas Iscariot, Simon's [son], which should betray him, Why was not this ointment sold for three hundred pence, and given to the poor? *This he said, not that he cared for the poor; but because he was a thief, and had the bag, and bare what was put therein.*[173]

"As I see it pastor John, Satan had so corrupted the mind of Judas through his covetousness that he was being used as a pawn to rob from Christ's ministry."

---

173 John 12:4-6.

"What you're saying professor is that Judas coveted after money and this opened a portal in his soul for Satan to enter. It caused him to err from his faith in Christ. How many fall for the love of money? How many times have you seen a wealthy man put only a few dollars in the collection plate? The love of money is a disease that has consequences worse than cancer." Jesus sums it up in Matthew where he says:

> *Lay not up for yourselves treasures upon earth, where moth and rust doth corrupt, and where thieves break through and steal: But lay up for yourselves treasures in heaven, where neither moth nor rust doth corrupt, and where thieves do not break through nor steal. For where your treasure is, there will your heart be also.*[174]

LINK 34: Sold out for Silver

"Pastor, Jesus did what he could to reprove Judas of his covetousness for money but Judas would not be swayed. But for Judas, it wasn't the money alone that he coveted. Judas had long hoped that Jesus would soon establish His kingdom on Earth. Judas had visions of greatness in Christ's new ruling government. He had the lust of the pride of life. He wanted to be important. So he decided to sell Jesus out for silver with the confident belief that Jesus would never die at the hands of His captors. Judas wanted to speed up the establishment of Christ's new kingdom and he believed his traitorous act would force Jesus to demonstrate His power."

---

174 Matthew 6:19-21.

SOLD FOR SILVER: The rulers purchased the Deliverer of Israel for silver. Delilah sold out Samson to the Philistines and Judas sold out Jesus to the Pharisees.

As the Scriptures record:

> *Then entered Satan into Judas surnamed Iscariot, being*
> *of the number of the twelve. And he went his way, and*

communed with the <u>chief priests and captains</u>, how he might betray him unto them. And they were glad, and covenanted to give him money. And he promised, and sought opportunity to betray him unto them in the absence of the multitude.[175]

"Likewise, the Lords of the Philistines covenanted with Delilah for money."

And the <u>lords of the Philistines</u> came up unto her, and said unto her, Entice him, and see wherein his great strength [lieth], and by what [means] we may prevail against him, that we may bind him to afflict him: and we will give thee every one of us eleven hundred [pieces] of silver.[176]

"Even the night when Judas brought the mob to take Jesus captive, Judas was confident that Jesus would show His glory. And for a moment it appeared that Christ would show His power. In the early moments of the confrontation, Jesus glory shone through and His captors fell back in astonishment and fear." As the Scriptures record:

Jesus therefore, knowing all things that should come upon him, went forth, and said unto them, Whom seek ye? They answered him, Jesus of Nazareth. Jesus saith unto them, I am [he]. And Judas also, which betrayed him, stood with them. As soon then as he had said unto them, I am [he], <u>they went backward, and fell to the ground.</u>[177]

"Pastor, the divinity of Jesus flashed out of Him like a glowing flash of energy and the crowd went backward and fell to the ground. Jesus was the *I Am* of the angel at Samson's birth. He was the I Am that appeared to Moses in the burning bush and the

---

175 Luke 22:3-6.
176 Judges 16:5.
177 John 18:4-6.

Angel in the Pillar Cloud that led Israel across the Red Sea.[178]
When the mob tried to take Jesus captive in the garden, all fell in
astonishment as the glory of His supernatural Being shone through.
But in the end, they bound Jesus and took Him captive, just as they
took Samson captive."

*When the morning was come, all the chief priests and
elders of the people took counsel against Jesus to put him
to death: And when they had bound him, they led [him]
away, and delivered him to Pontius Pilate the governor.
Then Judas, which had betrayed him, when he saw that
he was condemned, repented himself, and brought again
the thirty pieces of silver to the chief priests and elders,
Saying, I have sinned in that I have betrayed the innocent
blood. And they said, What [is that] to us? see thou [to
that]. And he cast down the pieces of silver in the temple,
and departed, and went and hanged himself. And the
chief priests took the silver pieces, and said, It is not
lawful for to put them into the treasury, because it is the
price of blood. And they took counsel, and bought with
them the potter's field, to bury strangers in. Wherefore
that field was called, The field of blood, unto this day.
Then was fulfilled that which was spoken by Jeremy the
prophet, saying, And they took the thirty pieces of silver,
the price of him that was valued, whom they of the
children of Israel did value; And gave them for the
potter's field, as the Lord appointed me.[179]*

"And these scenes were faithfully recorded in advance by the
prophet Zechariah."

*And I said unto them, If ye think good, give [me] my
price; and if not, forbear. So they weighed for my price
thirty [pieces] of silver. And the LORD said unto me,
Cast it unto the potter: a goodly price that I was prised at*

---

178 1 Corinthians 10:1-4.
179 Matthew 27:1-10.

of them. And I took the thirty [pieces] of silver, and cast them to the potter in the house of the LORD. [180]

And if you study the Scriptures carefully, you'll find that Joseph, another figure of Christ was also sold for silver. Thus, Samson, Joseph, and Jesus are tied together by this Golden Key. All three were sold *for the "love" of money.*

Event Sequence Analysis

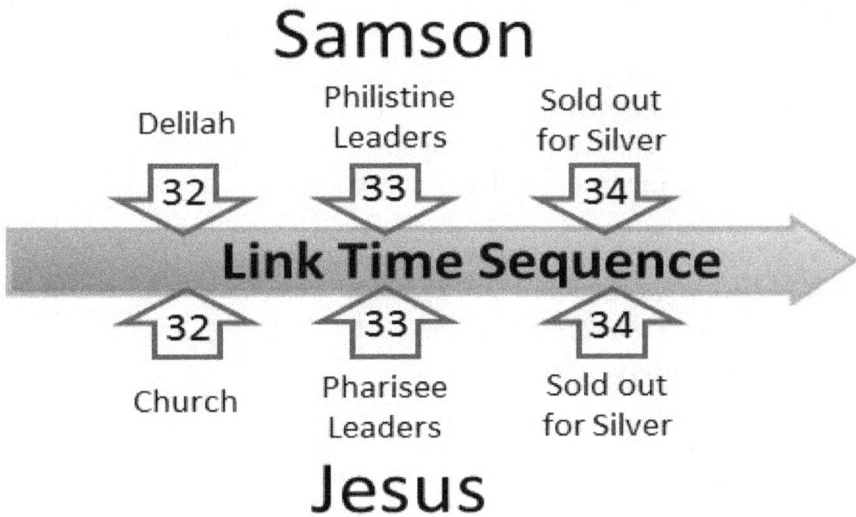

Samson

Delilah — Philistine Leaders — Sold out for Silver
32 — 33 — 34

Link Time Sequence

32 — 33 — 34
Church — Pharisee Leaders — Sold out for Silver

Jesus

---

180 Zechariah 11:12, 13.

11 *His Secret Power*

God came from Teman, and the Holy One from mount Paran. Selah. His glory covered the heavens, and the earth was full of his praise. And [his] brightness was as the light; he had horns [coming] out of his hand: and there [was] the hiding of his power. [Habakkuk 3:3, 4].

Then we turned to the subject of Samson's hair. "Professor, I'm curious about Samson's hair. If *the lust of money* is the second weapon, then what is the third? Does it have to do with Samson's hair?" "Yes pastor, but we have more to discover before we can discuss the riddle of Samson's hair. Trace the Scriptures and consider what happens next in the lives of Samson and Jesus." So the pastor quickly read aloud our list:

- *They were both born under foreign rule,*
- *An angel announced their births first to their mothers,*
- *They were both miracle babies,*
- *They were to be used of God from birth,*
- *Both would be Deliverers of Israel,*
- *An angel announced their births next to their fathers,*
- *The angel called himself "I AM" just as Jesus had,*
- *Samson's name means "Like the Sun,"*
- *Both were moved by the Spirit to do battle with the enemy,*
- *Both were tempted,*
- *Both sought the bride,*
- *Both defeated the roaring lion,*

- *Both begin their missions with a wedding,*
- *Both send them out two by two*
- *Both set the fields or should we say the world on fire,*
- *The gates of Hell cannot prevail against them,*
- *They carry the gate to the top of the hill or Calvary,*
- *Delilah and Judas betrayed the love of both Samson and Jesus,*
- *The Pharisees and Philistines plot to kill them, and*
- *Both were sold out for silver*

"Then what happens next pastor? Look for a thread common to both!" So he carefully traced the account in the Judges and smiled, "The text says his soul was vexed unto death!"

LINK 35: Soul Vexed to Death

"After Judas left the Upper Room to betray Jesus for silver, the apostles and disciples went to the garden and there Jesus left them to pray alone to the Father."

And saith unto them, <u>My soul is exceeding sorrowful unto death</u>: tarry ye here, and watch. And he went forward a little, and fell on the ground, and prayed that, if it were possible, the hour might pass from him.[181]

---

181 Mark 14:34, 35.

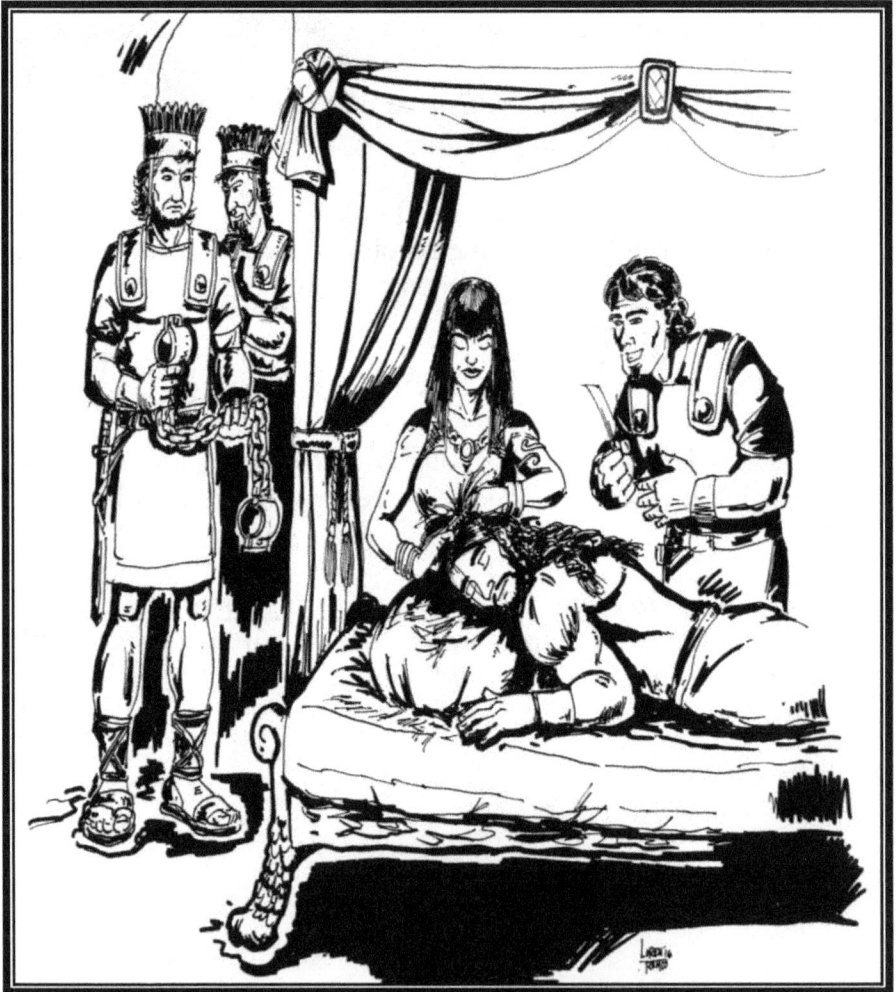

PUT HIMSELF IN THE HANDS OF THE WOMAN: Samson put his fate in the hands of the woman just as Jesus put His fate in the hands of the Church.

And with some excitement the pastor said, "this correlates with the passage in the Judges where it says: ***his soul was vexed unto death.***"[182]

"Yes pastor, both were vexed because of the woman. Samson was vexed by Delilah and Jesus was vexed by His Church and His bride; those whose burdens he carried. Both were willing to allow themselves to be taken captive because of love." It was as if scales had fallen from the pastor's eyes. He began to be convinced of the hidden messages. Then he said, "Samson knew that if he revealed the source of his power, she would betray him again. And this time the Lords of the Philistines would take him captive and they would kill him."

"Pastor, the situation was similar to that of Jesus. But the stress that Jesus carried for the love of the world was unimaginably more intense. He was being crushed like a grape as He began to take on the sins of the world. As Jesus prayed, drops of blood dripped from His forehead. It's as if He tasted His death on the Cross beforehand. He realized that the sins of man that He would carry would separate Him from God the Father. Jesus had been surrounded by darkness and satanic forces but He drew His strength and encouragement from the halls of heaven. After much prayer, Jesus was strengthened to continue. Jesus knew that Judas, His betrayer, would soon bring the Romans, the Pharisees, the chief priests, and the elders to take Him captive."

LINK 36: Lamb to Slaughter

As he scanned the text his eye fell upon the word razor. "Does the word razor convey a special meaning?"

> Strong's Concordance **04177 mowrah** {mo-raw'} in the sense of shearing; razor

"Yes," I replied. "If you look for the meaning in the Hebrew, you find that the word razor is used in the sense of shearing. You

---

182 Judges 16:16.

remember the text, and that ought to draw another connection for you."

> *All we like sheep have gone astray; we have turned every one to his own way; and the LORD hath laid on him [Jesus] the iniquity [sins] of us all. He [Jesus] was oppressed, and he was afflicted, yet he opened not his mouth: he is brought as a lamb to the slaughter, and as a sheep before her shearers.*[183]

It was the Lord that laid on Jesus the iniquity [sins] of us all. It was our sins that crushed Him. We each contributed to His death. And Jesus allowed Himself to carry our sins to save us.

Pride and Power

On that evening in the garden there was an intersection of earthly and supernatural forces. Angelic forces of Satan and angelic forces of Christ watched as the earthly war unfolded. Would the King of the universe be taken hostage or would He once again escape his enemies as he had on so many previous occasions?

Judas plotted to provoke a confrontation and reasoned that Jesus would finally show His Kingly stature. Judas was convinced that when Jesus would set up His earthly kingdom he would be given a position of prestige and power.

> *Now he that betrayed him gave them a sign, saying, Whomsoever I shall kiss, that same is he: hold him fast. And forthwith he came to Jesus, and said, Hail, master; and kissed him.*[184]

> *Jesus said unto him, Judas, betrayest thou the Son of man with a kiss?*[185]

---

183 Isaiah 53:6, 7.
184 Matthew 26:48, 49.
185 Luke 22:48.

And momentarily it appeared that Judas' plan to achieve power would unfold as he had hoped. As the Scriptures record:

> ***Jesus therefore, <u>knowing all things that should come upon him</u>, went forth, and said unto them, Whom seek ye? They answered him, Jesus of Nazareth. Jesus saith unto them, I am [he]. And Judas also, which betrayed him, stood with them. As soon then as he had said unto them, I am [he], <u>they went backward, and fell to the ground.</u>*** [186]

When Jesus greeted the mob His glory and righteousness flashed as light causing them to fall backward to the ground. Momentarily, it appeared that Christ's forces would once again drive away the enemy. A sword from Christ's forces was the first to draw blood.

> ***And one of them smote the servant of the high priest, and cut off his right ear.*** [187]

The opposing multitude was armed with swords and staves and a battle might have ensued had Jesus not intervened.

> ***And Jesus answered and said, Suffer ye thus far. And he touched his ear, and healed him.*** [188]

Jesus could have engaged the stunned multitude, seen and unseen, with His angelic hosts.

> ***Thinkest thou that I cannot now pray to my Father, and he shall presently give me more than twelve legions of angels?*** [189]

Jesus could have driven Satan and his forces away just as He did in heaven. [190]

---

186 John 18:4-6.
187 Luke 22:49, 50.
188 Luke 22:51.
189 Matthew 26:53.

but all this was done, that the scriptures of the prophets might be fulfilled.[191]

So in the end, Jesus allowed Himself to be taken prisoner and be bound just as was Samson. But things would end very badly for Judas.

Then Judas, which had betrayed him, when he saw that he was condemned, repented himself, and brought again the thirty pieces of silver to the chief priests and elders, Saying, I have sinned in that I have betrayed the innocent blood. And they said, What [is that] to us? see thou [to that]. And he cast down the pieces of silver in the temple, and departed, and went and hanged himself.[192] **Pride [goeth] before destruction, and an haughty spirit before a fall.**[193]

"You might say that the sin that brought about the end for both Judas and Satan was covetousness of pride and power. Satan like Judas wanted to raise himself above the throne of God. But in the end he will be destroyed."

LINK 37: Riddle of the 7 Locks

"But what about Samson's power and the shaving of his seven locks? What's the connection to Christ?"

"A very important connection!" I replied. "Maybe more important than many of the others we've discussed." The pastor had a distant look on his face as if lost in thought. He was searching his mind to find the connection. Then I began to ask the pastor a series of questions to lead him to the answer. "At this point in the sequence of events, where are the locks addressed?" And the pastor pointed to Judges 16:19 which reads:

---

190 Revelation 12:9.
191 Matthew 26:56.
192 Matthew 27:3-5.
193 Proverbs 16:18.

And she made him sleep upon her knees; and she called for a man, and she caused him to shave off the seven locks of his head; and she began to afflict him, and his strength went from him.[194]

"And what event does that precede?" "Samson put his head on the lap of the woman." "Yes, just as Jesus put His fate in the hands of the Church."

"What does that mean?"

"It implies that Jesus set aside His power right before they bound Him and took Him to the High Priest. But how does that align with Samson's seven locks?"

He was oppressed, and he was afflicted, yet he opened not his mouth: he is brought as a lamb to the slaughter, and as a sheep before her shearers is dumb, so he openeth not his mouth.[195]

"Sheep put their trust in the hands of those that shear them and this connection extends the parallels between Jesus as the Lamb of God."

"You're right, Jesus did temporarily lay down His power just after He showed them that He had all the power needed to knock them off their feet and make them momentarily senseless. But He didn't abuse His power."

"Jesus is the King of Kings and Lord of Lords. As King, what would symbolize His power?" "His crown?" He flipped through his Bible and pointed to the following passage:

And I saw heaven opened, and behold a white horse; and he that sat upon him [was] called Faithful and True, and in righteousness he doth judge and make war. His eyes [were] as a flame of fire, and on his head [were] many

---

194 Judges 16:9.
195 Isaiah 53:7.

crowns; and he had a name written, that no man knew, but he himself. And he [was] clothed with a vesture dipped in blood: and his name is called The Word of God. And he hath on [his] vesture and on his thigh a name written, KING OF KINGS, AND LORD OF LORDS.[196]

"Yes, the crown is a symbol of power and it's worn on the head of the King but we still haven't made the connection." The pastor stared off into space in deep concentration and then asked, "What else could it be?"

"Well pastor, we just concluded that both Jesus and Samson were led like sheep to the slaughter, right?" He nodded in agreement and said, "Jesus is the Lamb of God!"

"So where do we capture a picture of Jesus as the Lamb of God?" I asked. "He was called the lamb that was slain from the foundation of the earth." "You're getting closer," I replied. So I pointed to another text which reads:

And I beheld, and, lo, in the midst of the throne and of the four beasts, and in the midst of the elders, stood <u>a Lamb as it had been slain, having seven horns and seven eyes, which are the seven Spirits of God</u> sent forth into all the earth.[197]

"You see pastor, Jesus is the lamb slain from the foundation of the world with seven horns and seven eyes. Seven means completeness, and a horn is a symbol of power. Therefore He is all powerful or "*OMNIPOTENT.*" Likewise, the seven eyes convey that Jesus is all seeing or "*OMNISCIENT.*" *<u>And the seven horns are like the seven locks of Samson.</u>*"

"I understand," he smiled. "Wow! Is that it?"

---

196 Revelation 19:11-13, 16.
197 Revelation 5:6.

"Not completely, but we'll come back and unlock it's even deeper significance a little later. Samson lost his supernatural power that was given to him as a part of his Nazarite vows because he disobeyed God." "By contrast, Jesus gave up his connection to heavenly power to prove that He was willing to go through His period of suffering as a man." "Yes, He could have called on angels at any time, and He could have come down from the Cross but He was fulfilling the Scriptures. If Jesus used His supernatural powers, His Plan of Salvation would have failed and mankind would be forever lost."

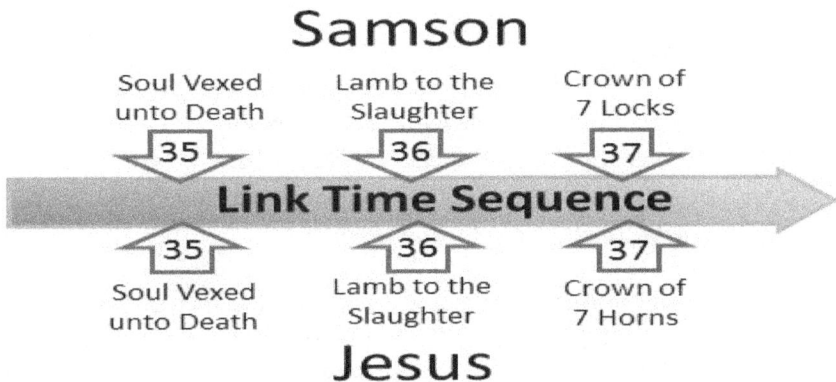

Samson

Soul Vexed unto Death	Lamb to the Slaughter	Crown of 7 Locks
35	36	37

Link Time Sequence

35	36	37
Soul Vexed unto Death	Lamb to the Slaughter	Crown of 7 Horns

Jesus

"If Jesus made a miss-step, God's kingdom would have come crashing down. Satan would do everything he could to get Jesus to make a mistake but in the end Satan lost the battle. And as the Scriptures attest, Jesus won the war through the weapon of LOVE."

12 *Blinded, Bound, and Imprisoned*

And the men that held Jesus mocked him, and smote [him]. And when they had blindfolded him, they struck him on the face [Luke 22:63, 64].

S atan had worked relentlessly for this moment. Jesus was now Satan's hostage. Samson and Jesus were allowed by the Halls of Heaven to fall into the clutches of the enemy, as Satan and his minions rejoiced. Satan was unaware that in both cases it was part of God's grand plan to deliver Israel. Jesus had been bound, blindfolded, and imprisoned like Samson before Him. The war between supernatural forces that began in heaven came to Planet Earth. It was a war that had been raging for thousands of years before Jesus' incarnation:

> *And there was war in heaven: Michael and his angels fought against the dragon; and the dragon fought and his angels, and prevailed not; neither was their place found any more in heaven. And the great dragon was cast out, that old serpent, called the Devil, and Satan, which deceiveth the whole world: he was cast out into the earth, and his angels were cast out with him.*[198]

Finally, after having been isolated to Planet Earth for thousands of years, the moment had arrived. Satan had, at least momentarily, been vindicated in front of his evil legions of angels for they had finally taken the King of the opposing forces captive.

---

198 Revelation 12:7-9.

Satan will use all his devices to bring down a man set on a mission by God. Untold thousands have been martyred in the service of God. And you and I are relentlessly under attack so:

> *be sober, be vigilant; because your adversary the devil, as a roaring lion, walketh about, seeking whom he may devour.[199]*

In Samson's case, Satan held the man of God like a lion clutching its prey. He knew that Samson was a man that God intended to use for His glory. It made Satan gleeful, at least for the moment for he thought that by sacrificing the Holy One he could undermine the Godhead's plan.

At Samson's birth, Satan and his evil forces eagerly listened to the conversations between Samson's parents and the secret I AM. And Satan and his demons are listening to you. They knew that the angel was Jesus, just as they recognized Jesus when He confronted the demoniac:

> *And there was in their synagogue a man with an unclean spirit; and he cried out, Saying, Let [us] alone; what have we to do with thee, thou Jesus of Nazareth? art thou come to destroy us? I know thee who thou art, the Holy One of God. And Jesus rebuked him, saying, Hold thy peace, and come out of him.[200]*

Samson had been raised as a man of God from birth, yet he was so infatuated and so enfeebled by Delilah that he finally abandoned his Nazarite vows and gave her the secret to his great strength. In the moment of his weakness Samson had unwittingly given up his heavenly mission to deliver Israel, or so one would think.

But God allowed his capture to serve as the prophetic foreshadowing of the capture of the true Deliverer of Israel, Jesus Christ.

---

199 1 Peter 5:8.
200 Mark 1:23-25.

In Christ's case, Satan was sure that he finally held the Messiah in his grasp. For the previous three years, Satan had lost one battle after another. Satan was embarrassed in the wilderness when Christ overcame his temptations. But Satan finally found the key to Christ's weakness. Jesus fell for the love of a woman, His bride, the Church. But in all of Satan's glee he didn't realize that the tables would soon be turned upon his head.[201]Like Samson, Christ's birth was announced by a multitude of angels as the long awaited Deliverer of Israel. Once again Satan and his evil forces had carefully listened to the conversations between the shepherds and the angels. Christ had been raised as the Son of God from birth, yet he was so enfeebled by His love for the lost sheep of Israel, the bride of Christ, that He willingly set aside His heavenly powers to allow the Plan of Salvation to be fulfilled. In contrast to Samson, Christ was determined to fulfill the mission that was established from the foundation of the world. He would die so that many would be saved. But the secret to the Plan was still in place:

> *for none of the princes of this world knew: for had they known [it], they would not have crucified the Lord of glory.*[202]

The princes of the world including the chief priests, the elders, the King, the High Priest, and the Roman Governor would not have crucified Him had they known that He was the Son of God. They wouldn't have dared. So they were left to make the choice based on their own hearts. And their true hearts were revealed.

LINK 38: Blinded

The pastor said as he pointed at the verses, "The connection between Samson and Christ are again clear in verse 21. The scripture says **they put out Samson's eyes** just as they blindfolded Jesus."

> *But the Philistines took him, and put out his eyes.*[203]

---

201 Psalm 7:16.
202 1 Corinthians 2:8.

"Likewise, Jesus was blindfolded."

> ***And when they had blindfolded him, they struck him on the face, and asked him, saying, Prophesy, who is it that smote thee?[204]***

"That's pretty simple," he concluded. "Well it's meaning is a lot deeper than that," I replied. "How so?" he asked.

"***You know***," and I hummed, "***I once was lost but now am found was blind but now I see***." Many have 20-20 vision but they're blind to the true meaning of the Scriptures. And that discernment is really a matter of your heart and your relationship to God. The Scriptures say:

> ***not as Moses, [which] put a veil over his face, that the children of Israel could not stedfastly look to the end of that which is abolished: But their minds were blinded: for until this day remaineth the same veil untaken away in the reading of the old testament; which [veil] is done away in Christ. But even unto this day, when Moses is read, the veil is upon their heart.[205]***

"You see pastor, many still have a mysterious supernatural veil over their hearts and are blind to the true meaning of the Scriptures and many are lost because they don't have spiritual vision."

LINK 39: Bound with Fetters of Brass

"And both Samson and Jesus were bound. It says that Samson was bound with fetters of brass. What do you make of that pastor?"

---

203 Judges 16:21.
204 Luke 22:64.
205 2 Corinthians 3:13-17.

"From a deeper perspective, it says to me that we're all bound in chains of sin."

I smiled in acknowledgement, "You can plainly see that Satan has bound humanity in chains of ignorance and sin. Satan uses our sins to condemn us to death for the wages of sin are death. As a result, most have given up all hope that there's a God and so they find the best comfort they can in the world. But in the end, the world can't provide them the answers and it can't offer them a means of escape from death."

"Then there's no hope for them," he sighed. "Pastor, death is a terrifying thought for unbelievers. They have no hope. If the roles were reversed and you were in their condition would you want someone to give you proof that God exists and that God sent His Son into the world to save them?" "Absolutely! I think I'm beginning to see what you're saying. We have a solemn obligation to give them the evidence to believe," he replied. The Scriptures tell us to take action:

> *Go ye therefore, and teach all nations, baptizing them in the name of the Father, and of the Son, and of the Holy Ghost: Teaching them to observe all things whatsoever I have commanded you: and, lo, I am with you alway, [even] unto the end of the world. Amen.*[206]

---

206 Matthew 28:19, 20.

BOTH WERE BOUND: Samson and Jesus were both laughed at, blinded (or blind-folded), bound, humiliated, and tortured.

"Pastor, we have to be so convincing that they'll have no excuse. If you read the Scriptures, we're told that:

> *the invisible things of him from the creation of the world are clearly seen, being understood by the things that are made, [even] his eternal power and Godhead; so that <u>they are without excuse</u>.*[207]

"As a scientist and geochemist, I bear a great burden pastor. I see that the whole world has been put under Satan's darkness. Satan has done great harm by twisting the minds of men like Darwin and Charles Lyell. Lyell preached that the world has changed little over the millennia. He taught a theory called uniformitarianism. And the Bible warned of that. "

"I've heard of the debates between creationists and evolutionists. I know that some churches even accept the theory of evolution. Where do you find uniformitarianism in the Scriptures? "

"Turn with me to Second Peter." There it says:

> *there shall come in the last days scoffers, walking after their own lusts, And saying, Where is the promise of his coming? for since the fathers fell asleep, <u>all things continue as [they were] from the beginning of the creation</u>.*[208]

"Notice that the Scriptures say that in the end of time scoffers will make fun of creationists saying that <u>***all things remain the same from the beginning***</u>. Scientists refer to things remaining the same as the theory of uniformitarianism. They use the slogan that "***the present is the key to the past***" to teach this theory. That is, they say that the processes and rates we see operating today are the same as those that were operating in the past. In other words, they believe that everything has operated uniformly since the beginning of time." The passage continues by saying:

---

207 Romans 1:20.
208 2 Peter 3:3, 4.

***For this they willingly are ignorant of, that by the word of
God the heavens were of old, and the earth standing out
of the water and in the water: Whereby the world that
then was, being overflowed with water, perished.*[209]**

"They don't believe in the Flood either because a cataclysmic
world-wide Flood defies uniformitarianism so they are willingly
ignorant of the Flood. After all, a worldwide Flood would
contradict the theory of uniformitarianism. Scientists even fought
against the Missoula Floods of the Columbia Basin in Washington
State but that flooding is now widely accepted by the scientific
community."

"Do you believe in a world-wide flood?" "I wouldn't rule it out.
There's a lot of evidence for the Flood." "Then you need to write
down all that you've told me in a book and share it with the
world." "I'm working on it pastor, and you're helping a great deal
today."

"Humanity has been misled by Darwin to believe that the Flood
and Creation are just myths. Frankly, for that reason, most don't
believe in God. And the Scriptures tell us that many will fall under
the delusion of uniformitarianism and not believe in Creationism.
But the account of Christ hidden behind the account of Samson
written more than a thousand years in advance provides the
evidence that God exists. It's undeniable." "I agree."

LINK 40: Imprisoned

"Pastor, we're all imprisoned in this world and there's no way out.
We're all doomed to death and the grave because all have been
mortally wounded; all have sinned and fallen short and the wages
of sin is death. Jesus is our only hope! And Jesus, through the
lens of Samson, carried the prison gate to the top of the hill. The
gate to the prison house has been removed at the Cross on the Hill
of Calvary. Jesus has made a Way of escape from the grave."

---

209 2 Peter 3:5, 6.

"The Scriptures tell us that Jesus came **to open the blind eyes, to bring out the prisoners from the prison, [and] them that sit in darkness out of the prison house.**"[210]

LINK 41: He did Grind

"So Don, what does it mean that "**he will grind in the prison house?**" "Pastor, focus on the words "**he will grind**" for a moment." Jesus said:

> **And whosoever shall fall on this stone shall be broken: but on whomsoever it shall fall, it will grind him to powder.**[211]

"I get it Don. Grinding is a means by which grain was ground to separate the wheat from the chaff. Metaphorically, Jesus is the corner stone. Each of us like grain is ground upon the rock and that Rock is Jesus. He wants to get rid of our chaff. Jesus wants us to be purified so He subjects us to trials and suffering to show us that evil exists in our characters. We must be broken open like the kernels of grain that we can be separated from the chaff, which is the sin in our characters. We must be separated from the desires that lead us to associate with the wickedness of the world like our pride, our lusts, our idol worship, and our passions. We can only overcome by the grace of Jesus. Like the grain, Jesus is our means of being broken of our worldly desires. Only by walking closely with Jesus can we grind away our sinful desires."

"So how does this apply to the connection between Samson and Jesus?" He asked.

"Well again, Samson represents the physical and Jesus represents the supernatural. Samson was physically grinding grain, whereas Jesus was supernaturally separating the wheat from the chaff. In those bitter hours the rulers and people were separating their own destinies into two camps: those that believed in Him and those that

210 Isaiah 42:7.
211 Matthew 21:44.

accused Him. Jesus let the people decide for themselves. If Jesus had come down from the Cross everyone would have sided with Him out of fear."

"Satan easily worked through those that were undecided and let his fallen angels occupy them as trophies of war. And they cried out through their captives "Crucify Him, Crucify Him" just as Satan had entered into Judas. Meanwhile, those that believed in Him mourned and suffered. Each one present was given the free will to decide who they would follow. Even Pilate was given the choice. But even though Pilate wanted to find an excuse to free Jesus, because he'd been warned by his wife's dream, he ultimately allowed the crucifixion to proceed. " According to the Scriptures:

> *When Pilate saw that he could prevail nothing, but [that] rather a tumult was made, he took water, and washed [his] hands before the multitude, saying, I am innocent of the blood of this just person: see ye [to it]. Then answered all the people, and said, His blood [be] on us, and on our children.*[212]

"And their prophecy was fulfilled. Even under great stress, Jesus was separating the wheat from the chaff. And we today are being separated into two camps; those that will follow Jesus and those that will follow the way of Satan and his fallen world. And you'll note that only a few choose to follow Jesus just as only a few chose to enter Noah's Ark."

"So we need to allow our characters to be cleansed of the evils that Satan has contaminated us with that we might escape doom and death."

"Today the world has been led astray and many are without hope unless we share the Light of Jesus with them. Satan, his legions of angels, and unwitting human agents are mixing the chaff of error with the wheat of truth. They are corrupting science and religion to drive people even further from the Scriptures."

---

212 Matthew 27:24, 25.

"Today, many are even embarrassed to read a Bible and if they continue to be ashamed. Jesus says:"

> *Whosoever therefore shall be ashamed of me and of my words in this adulterous and sinful generation; of him also shall the Son of man be ashamed, when he cometh in the glory of his Father with the holy angels.*[213]

"What about the prison house? I understand that both Jesus and Samson were imprisoned but I'm certain that there's a deeper meaning?" the pastor replied. "What do you think Don?"

LINK 42: Satan Rejoiced at His Capture

"What do you see in the verses that follow pastor?" I asked. And the pastor read the verses:

> *Then the lords of the Philistines gathered them together for to offer a great sacrifice unto Dagon their god, and to <u>rejoice</u>: for they said, Our god hath delivered Samson our enemy into our hand. And when the people saw him, they praised their god: for they said, Our god hath delivered into our hands our enemy, and the destroyer of our country, which slew many of us.*[214]

"Who is Dagon?" I asked. "He's the god of the Philistines. I remember the passage from first Samuel." The passage says:

Strong's Concordance 01712
Dagown {daw-gohn'}
Dagon = "a fish" 1) a Philistine deity of fertility; represented with the face and hands of a man and the tail of a fish.

---

213 Mark 8:38.
214 Judges 16:23, 24.

the Philistines took the ark of God, they brought it into the house of Dagon, and set it by Dagon. And when they of Ashdod arose early on the morrow, behold, Dagon [was] fallen upon his face to the earth before the ark of the LORD. And they took Dagon, and set him in his place again. And when they arose early on the morrow morning, behold, Dagon [was] fallen upon his face to the ground before the ark of the LORD; and the head of Dagon and both the palms of his hands [were] cut off upon the threshold; only [the stump of] Dagon was left to him.[215]

LINK 43: Great Sacrifice

Then I asked again, "Pastor, if you compare the account of Samson to the account of Jesus you realize that both are sacrifices." The pastor found the point in the text that reads:

Then the lords of the Philistines gathered them together for to offer a <u>great sacrifice</u> unto Dagon their god, and to rejoice: for they said, Our god hath delivered Samson our enemy into our hand. [216]

"The Philistines had finally captured Samson and they were going to offer him up as a great sacrifice to their false god Dagon. Do you see the parallel?"

"Yes Don, if the Philistines considered Samson to be a great sacrifice how much greater would the sacrifice of the one we refer to as Jesus be? Jesus didn't have to leave the throne of heaven to save the world from sin. But in His infinite love, He stepped down from that throne with an infinite measure of self-denial and self-sacrifice. His was the ultimate measure of love." "Yes pastor. Jesus was the greatest sacrifice. Samson's sacrifice pales by comparison."

---

215 1 Samuel 5:1-4.
216 Judges 16:23.

DAGON A SYMBOL OF SATAN: Dagon, symbolized as a fish god would fall to Samson, just as Satan would fall to Jesus.

LINK 44: Dagon symbol of Satan

Then I asked again, "Pastor, if you compare the account of Samson to the account of Jesus, who does Dagon symbolize?" *"It can only be Satan."* He exclaimed. "Satan and his fallen angels rejoiced at the capture of Jesus just as the Philistines rejoiced at the capture of Samson. And Dagon fell on his face and was destroyed in the presence of the ark of the God of Israel." "What happened to the ark of the God of Israel?" "They let it go from their clutches. Because the text says:

> *So they sent and gathered together all the lords of the Philistines, and said, Send away the ark of the God of Israel, and let it go again to his own place, that it slay us not, and our people: for there was a deadly destruction throughout all the city; the hand of God was very heavy there.*[217]

"How does this apply to the account of Jesus?" "It must have been Satan that was behind the trial and crucifixion of Jesus. But where do we find the crucifixion of Jesus in the account of Samson?"

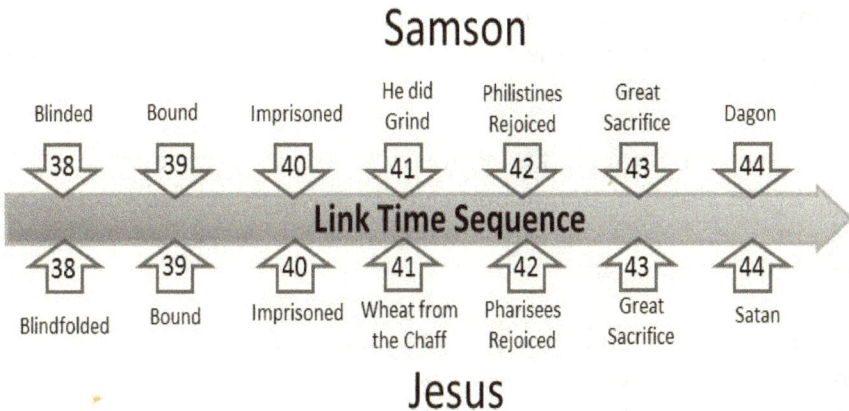

---

217 1 Samuel 5:11.

13 *Victory at the Cross-road*

I know thy works, and tribulation, and poverty, (but thou art rich) and [I know] the blasphemy of them which say they are Jews, and are not, but [are] the synagogue of Satan.[218]

We were mid-way through Glacier National Park. Time was running by. Well pastor, we've arrived at the climax of the account of Samson. By studying, sifting, and comparing the accounts of Samson and Jesus, a clearer view of the victory that God wrought will open unto you." "I could never have imagined Samson as a type of Christ. I knew that in the end He delivered Israel. But it wasn't until he was taken captive that he finally reached out to God."

"Samson was destined to be God's anointed vessel that would accomplish the deliverance of Israel out of the hands of the Philistines. The Philistines had been the medium through which Satan worked to undermine the Divine mission of God. But it was God Himself that allowed Satan to use the Philistines for forty years to reprove Israel and turn them back to Him. During those forty years, the Philistines had seen mighty conquests that they attributed to their fish God, Dagon. They were confident that Dagon was superior to the God of Israel. Little did they know that the tables would soon be turned."

"God worked through the Philistines to far more than reprove Israel. He also used the opportunity to show to the Philistines, the Israelites, and each one of us today that He is the One and only true God."

"When Samson had finally been taken captive, a feast was proclaimed in honor of Dagon who had wrought a mighty work by delivering the Philistine's enemy, Samson, into their hands.

---

218 Revelation 2:9.

Samson had been a continual thorn in the side of the Philistines and they held him helpless in their clutches, or so they thought."

"On an unseen level, the revelers were joined by Satan and his host of fallen angels who were celebrating the victory that they thought was to the credit of their leader Satan. Satan and his followers thought that it was through their own powers and cunning that they had taken captive one of God's elect, just as in the account of the stolen Ark of the Covenant. But the capture of Samson, like the Ark, was allowed by God to be used as a *Trojan horse*. For when Samson was taken captive, God planned a mighty victory over Satan and his forces. God would use Samson, His anointed, just as He did with the captured Ark. Samson was now the Trojan Horse in the camp of Satan."

"The entire celebration foreshadowed the capture of Jesus Christ more than a thousand years into the future. When Jesus was captured, untold numbers of fallen angels clamored in glee as Jesus was finally taken into their clutches. They viewed Jesus as the head of the enemy legions that had cast Satan and his fallen angels out of heaven and they wanted revenge. God would work a mighty victory through His only begotten Son. And in the parallel, victory would be brought about through the death of Samson, whose name means "Like the Son," as a prophetic sign of the victory that would later be wrought through His Only Begotten Son. And for the moment at least, the two captives, Samson and Jesus, seemed helpless and defenseless in the clutches of their enemies."

"But the God of Israel is, and ever will be the all-powerful, omnipotent God of His Universe."

"The Philistines and Pharisees alike defied the God of Israel and unwittingly and unknowingly raised Dagon above the God of Israel. The Pharisees unwittingly were working as vessels for Satan. Their own pride, envy, greed, and a myriad of other flawed character traits allowed Satan's fallen angels to enter them as evil channels. And it was through them that Satan worked the crowd into anger against Christ just as Satan had worked the crowd into anger against Samson. And when Pilate finally brought Jesus and

Barabbas before the crowd they were likewise exceedingly agitated. Pilate set forth a clear choice for them."

> *The governor answered and said unto them, Whether of the twain will ye that I release unto you? They said, Barabbas. Pilate saith unto them, What shall I do then with Jesus which is called Christ? [They] all say unto him, Let him be crucified. And the governor said, Why, what evil hath he done? But they cried out the more, saying, Let him be crucified. When Pilate saw that he could prevail nothing, but [that] rather a tumult was made, he took water, and washed [his] hands before the multitude, saying, I am innocent of the blood of this just person: see ye [to it].[219]*

> *But Pilate answered them, saying, Will ye that I release unto you the King of the Jews? For he knew that <u>the chief priests had delivered him for envy</u>. But the chief priests moved the people, that he should rather release Barabbas unto them. And Pilate answered and said again unto them, What will ye then that I shall do [unto him] whom ye call the King of the Jews? And they cried out again, Crucify him.[220]*

"Pilate knew that the chief priests had delivered Jesus for envy. For it was envy and pride manifested through the vengeful character of Satan that once again manifested itself through the faces in the crowd. And when Pilate asked what they would have him do, the evil angels shouted through the mob of thousands, *"Crucify Him! Crucify Him!"* in blood curdling screams through the mouths of their hapless victims. Yes, Satan's angels worked as body snatchers."

"And so Pilate, in order to appease the angry crowd and keep them from rioting, had Jesus scourged and then released Him to be crucified. Had the Pharisees, studied the sacred Scriptures, they

---

219 Matthew 27:21-24.
220 Mark 15:9-13.

would have realized that they were the focus of the prophetic words of Isaiah (Isaiah 53:1-12) and they would have stopped the celebration. Had they studied the sign of Jonah or so many other prophetic proclamations about the trial, they would have seen that the tables were soon to be turned. But a dark veil was pulled over their hearts and minds so that they couldn't see that they were being manipulated by Satan."

"Likewise, the captors of Samson celebrated his capture. Shouts of victory swept through the crowd. Thousands of men and fallen angels exulted at the victory that they attributed to Dagon. The crowds swelled within and upon the synagogue of Dagon."

> *Now the house was full of men and women; and all the lords of the Philistines [were] there; and [there were] upon the roof about three thousand men and women, that beheld while Samson made sport.*[221]

"Pastor, imagine, there were three thousand on the roof alone. In both cases the scene was of an enormous, tumultuous crowd reveling in their victory."

"And so Samson was called out to be taunted and tormented by the angry mob, just as Jesus would be mocked and spat upon. Samson, by divine design, walked step by step, as if choreographing the walk of Jesus more than a thousand years in advance."

"After the crowd made sport of Samson, he asked the young lad that held his hand to let him lean upon the two main pillars of the temple as the crowd continued to mock him and wag their tongues. Likewise, Christ was bound to the Cross as they wagged their tongues at Him."

"And in those most miserable moments Samson would cry out to the God of Israel just as Jesus would later cry out. Samson prayed, and *"called unto the LORD, and said, O Lord GOD, remember*

---

221 Judges 16:27.

me, I pray thee, and strengthen me, I pray thee,"[222] just as the Psalmist prayed, **"Remember me, O LORD, with the favour [that thou bearest unto] thy people: O visit me with thy salvation; That I may see the good of thy <u>chosen</u>, that I may rejoice in the gladness of <u>thy nation</u>, that I may glory with <u>thine inheritance</u>.**"[223]

"And likewise, Jesus a thousand years into the future would call out as foretold by the Psalmist."

> *My God, my God, why hast thou forsaken me? [why art thou so] far from helping me, [and from] the words of my roaring?*"[224] **(Psalm 22:1).** *I will say unto God my rock, Why hast thou forgotten me? why go I mourning because of the oppression of the enemy? [As] with a sword in my bones, mine enemies reproach me; while they say daily unto me, Where [is] thy God? Why art thou cast down, O my soul? and why art thou disquieted within me? hope thou in God: for I shall yet praise him, [who is] the health of my countenance, and my God.*"[225] *"And about the ninth hour Jesus cried with a loud voice, saying, Eli, Eli, lama sabachthani? that is to say, My God, my God, why hast thou forsaken me?*[226]

"The contest, instead of being between Samson and the Philistines, was always between Jesus and Satan, and thus the Lord was moved to assert His almighty power and His supreme authority. Nothing in the Old Testament represents the trial and punishment of Jesus as the fifty-third chapter of Isaiah," the pastor concluded. "They made sport of Jesus just as they did Samson." So he turned to the text and read the verses:

> *He is despised and rejected of men; a man of sorrows, and acquainted with grief: and we hid as it were [our] faces*

---

222 Judges 16:28.
223 Psalm 106:4, 5.
224 Psalm 22:1.
225 Psalm 42:9-11.
226 Matthew 27:46.

from him; he was despised, and we esteemed him not. Surely he hath borne our griefs, and carried our sorrows: yet we did esteem him stricken, smitten of God, and afflicted. But he [was] wounded for our transgressions, [he was] bruised for our iniquities: the chastisement of our peace [was] upon him; and with his stripes we are healed. All we like sheep have gone astray; we have turned every one to his own way; and the LORD hath laid on him the iniquity of us all. He was oppressed, and he was afflicted, yet he opened not his mouth: he is brought as a lamb to the slaughter, and as a sheep before her shearers is dumb, so he openeth not his mouth. He was taken from prison and from judgment: and who shall declare his generation? for he was cut off out of the land of the living: for the transgression of my people was he stricken. And he made his grave with the wicked, and with the rich in his death; because he had done no violence, neither [was any] deceit in his mouth. Yet it pleased the LORD to bruise him; he hath put [him] to grief: when thou shalt make his soul an offering for sin, he shall see [his] seed, he shall prolong [his] days, and the pleasure of the LORD shall prosper in his hand. He shall see of the travail of his soul, [and] shall be satisfied: by his knowledge shall my righteous servant justify many; for he shall bear their iniquities. Therefore will I divide him [a portion] with the great, and he shall divide the spoil with the strong; because he hath poured out his soul unto death: and he was numbered with the transgressors; and he bare the sin of many, and made intercession for the transgressors. [227]

"The battle between Christ and Satan and between Samson and Satan played out on the stage of the Universe. The messages of the Scriptures were faithfully and mysteriously written for all to see, yet the princes of the world, including the fallen angels, the Pharisees, the Romans and all those that crucified Jesus knew not

---

227 Isaiah 53:3-12.

what they were doing *"for had they known [it], they would not have crucified the Lord of glory."*[228]

"They had been given the free will to decide which side they would take. Their hearts would bear witness to the one that they would serve; whether it be Christ or Satan. You and I have been given the same choice. Who will you serve?"

LINK 45: Made Sport of Him

"The Passover was a time of large crowds made up of travelers from far and wide making their way to Jerusalem. The Pharisees and the other religious leaders finally held Jesus captive after three and a half years of constant confrontation. The truths that Christ had hurled at the Pharisees made their pride and envy swell to a feverish peak just days before as He had arrived in His Kingly procession into Jerusalem. They were humiliated even more when He drove the money changers from the Temple. Their pride escalated to a burning rage and once they held Jesus in captivity, they made sport of Him in retribution for the way he had lowered their status in the eyes of the people."

"Jesus had openly attacked the scribes and Pharisees in front of the vast crowds that followed Him saying:"

For they bind heavy burdens and grievous to be borne, and lay [them] on men's shoulders; but they [themselves] will not move them with one of their fingers. But all their works they do for to be seen of men: they make broad their phylacteries, and enlarge the borders of their garments, And love the uppermost rooms at feasts, and the chief seats in the synagogues, And greetings in the markets, and to be called of men, Rabbi, Rabbi. [Ye] serpents, [ye] generation of vipers, how can ye escape the damnation of hell? Wherefore, behold, I send unto you prophets, and wise men, and scribes: and [some] of them

---

228 1 Corinthians 2:7, 8.

ye shall kill and crucify; and [some] of them shall ye scourge in your synagogues, and persecute [them] from city to city: That upon you may come all the righteous blood shed upon the earth, from the blood of righteous Abel unto the blood of Zacharias son of Barachias, whom ye slew between the temple and the altar.[229]

"Needless to say, the Jewish leadership had been incensed with envy and anger by His strong accusations and attacks on their character. Worst of all, they feared that the multitudes would crown Him King of the Jews and they would lose their power and become His servants. And so it was that they plotted to kill Him. And now as He stood before them, held by the Roman authorities, they felt vindicated and reveled at His pain and grief. They now wanted Him to be punished for the cutting words that He had said. So, under the influence of Satan's army they worked up the crowd to cry out, Crucify Him! Crucify Him!"

"Likewise, the Philistines had numerous conflicts with Samson. He had burned their fields and taken their women. In the parallel, Jesus had set the Pharisees fields on fire and took their followers from them." *And it came to pass, when their hearts were merry, that they said, Call for Samson, that he may make us sport. And they called for Samson out of the prison house; and he made them sport: and they set him between the pillars.*[230]

LINK 46: Outstretched Arms

"When they nailed Jesus to the Cross His arms were outstretched, blood ran down His body from the scourging that He had received and from the crown of thorns that had pierced His head. To friend and enemy alike He looked helpless."

---

229 Matthew 23:4-7, 33-35.
230 Judges 16:25.

THE SHADOW OF CHRIST: *With his arms outstretched on the two pillars, Samson was foreshadowing the figure of Jesus with His arms outstretched on the Cross. Both would die victoriously and defeat the enemy.*

"But God's Plan to save mankind was still proceeding, uninterrupted by those in attendance." "Bound like a criminal, Samson made a request of his keeper."

And Samson said unto the lad that held him by the hand, Suffer me that I may feel the pillars whereupon the house standeth, that I may lean upon them. And Samson took hold of the two middle pillars upon which the house stood, and on which it was borne up, of the one with his right hand, and of the other with his left.[231]

"Both Jesus and Samson died with their arms outstretched."

LINK 47: Pray to God

"What do you see next pastor?" "Just before they die, both Samson and Jesus pray to God." "Yes pastor, and one requests that he be remembered. And the other asks that He not be forgotten."

And Samson called unto the LORD, and said, O Lord GOD, remember me, I pray thee, and strengthen me, I pray thee, only this once, O God, that I may be at once avenged of the Philistines for my two eyes.[232]

And at the ninth hour Jesus cried with a loud voice, saying, Eloi, Eloi, lama sabachthani? which is, being interpreted, My God, my God, why hast thou forsaken me?[233]

---

231 Judges 16:26, 29.
232 Judges 16:28.
233 Mark 15:34.

"You see, both had been separated from God. And now they both put their trust in the Father."

LINK 48: Destroys House of Dagon

"Pastor notice how the account proceeds."

And Samson took hold of the two middle pillars upon which the house stood, and on which it was borne up, of the one with his right hand, and of the other with his left. And Samson said, Let me die with the Philistines. And he bowed himself with [all his] might; and the house fell upon the lords, and upon all the people that [were] therein.

"And these two pillars have great significance. These are the two pillars that held up the Temple of Dagon, or should I say the Synagogue of Satan. Satan's synagogue is built on the pillar of sin and the pillar of death. The pillars of sin and death form the archway to Satan's kingdom. All that follow Satan will pass through his arch and suffer eternal death."

"In stark contrast, the two pillars of the Church of Christ are baptism and the Lord's supper, both symbolizing Christ's death burial, and resurrection. These two pillars represent the antidotes for sin and death. All who pass through this archway to the entrance to Christ's Church will be granted remission of sins and eternal life."

"So one doorway leads you to eternal death; the other leads you to eternal life."

"Yes pastor, when Samson stretched out his arms, with a mighty push he brought down the pillars upon the Philistines that were celebrating his capture. With his death, Samson brought down the

Temple of Dagon. In like fashion, when Jesus Christ, stretched out His arms and with a mighty effort He brought down the pillars of the Synagogue of Satan."

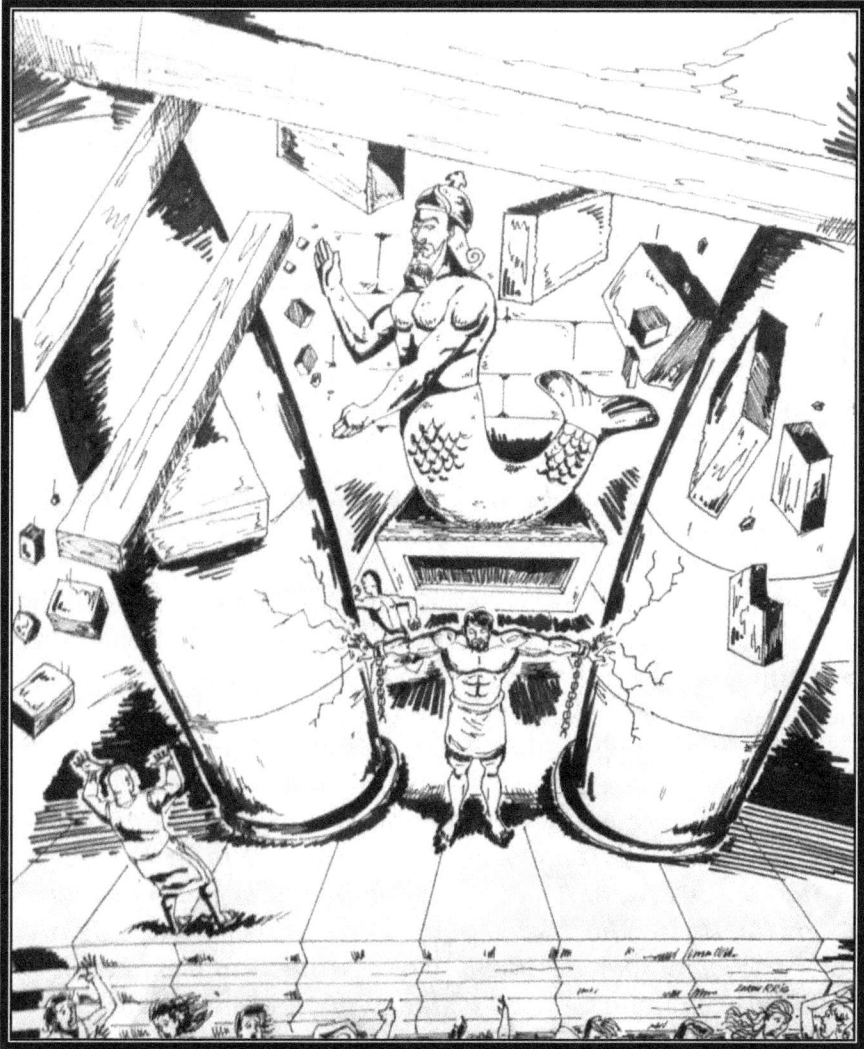

HE BROUGHT DOWN THE HOUSE OF SATAN OR DAGON:

Just as Samson brought down the House of Dagon, Jesus would likewise bring down the House of Satan.

So when this corruptible shall have put on incorruption, and this mortal shall have put on immortality, then shall be brought to pass the saying that is written, Death is swallowed up in victory. O death, where [is] thy sting? O grave, where [is] thy victory? The sting of death [is] sin; and the strength of sin [is] the law. But thanks [be] to God, which giveth us the victory through our Lord Jesus Christ.[234]

LINK 49: Slew More in Death than Life

"What does the text mean when it says:"

So the dead which he slew at his death were more than [they] which he slew in his life.[235]

I replied, "Pastor you know. Christ has killed more in death than in life! That is to say, metaphorically, He has killed our former evil, sinful selves and planted a new heart in us. Or putting it another way, He has converted millions." "Pastor, you know that the Book of Acts tells us that after the death of Christ:"

believers *were added to the Lord, multitudes both of men and women. Insomuch that they brought forth the sick into the streets, and laid [them] on beds and couches, that at the least the shadow of Peter passing by might overshadow some of them. There came also a multitude [out] of the cities round about unto Jerusalem, bringing sick folks, and them which were vexed with unclean spirits: and they were healed every one.*[236]

---

234 1 Corinthians 15:54-57.
235 Judges 16:30.
236 Acts 5:14-16.

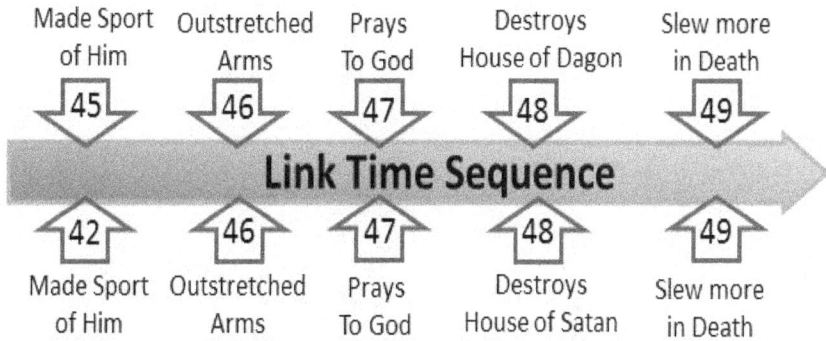

"You see pastor, when Samson turned away from the Lord, he lost the sight of both his eyes and his power. And that's another lesson for us. When we turn away from the Lord, we give ourselves into the hands of the enemy. When Samson's hair had grown back and he prayed unto the Lord, the Lord returned his strength that he might complete his mission to deliver Israel. Like Samson, each of us has been given a plan laid out by the Father. If we turn to Him, He will wash away our sins and give us the supernatural power to complete our missions."

"Samson had taken a sacred vow as a Nazarite, but when he broke his vow he lost his supernatural power. How many of us today take vows at the Lord's Supper or at our baptism only to walk away? In so doing we lose the power of the Holy Spirit."

"All along the Way, Jesus called on His Father and His prayers were answered. Jesus made us a sure archway to eternal life."

14 *Unlocking the 7 Sealed Book*

And I saw in the right hand of him that sat on the throne a book written within and on the backside, sealed with seven seals. [Revelation 5:1].

The pastor asked, "Is that the end of the story?" "No pastor, we've just arrived at a critical point in the timeline. It introduces a whole new phase of God's mercies." "New phase?" "We need to go back and review the events following the crucifixion of Christ to figure it out. We just left Samson under a pile of rubble and Jesus hanging on the Cross. What do you recall as the next events in their accounts?"

"The text says that they were both buried." "Yes! And then what?" "He judged Israel?" "True as well. But what happened between the burial of Jesus and His role as our Judge? The Scriptures tell us that the hour of His judgment is come."

> **And I saw another angel fly in the midst of heaven, having the everlasting gospel to preach unto them that dwell on the earth, and to every nation, and kindred, and tongue, and people, Saying with a loud voice, Fear God, and give glory to him; for the hour of his judgment is come: and worship him that made heaven, and earth, and the sea, and the fountains of waters.**[237]

"We are to preach the gospel and warn the world because He will soon return. Why? Because, the **treasures of darkness and hidden riches of secret places that had been sealed for ages were unlocked** soon after the victory was won at the Cross. And once

---

237 Revelation 14:6,7.

we see the treasures that were held secret for ages, we'll know without a doubt that the Lord, Jesus Christ is the God of Israel."

"What treasures?" "Remember pastor that the Scriptures tell us that Jesus spoke in a mysterious symbolic language."

> *All these things spake Jesus unto the multitude in parables; and without a parable spake he not unto them: That it might be fulfilled which was spoken by the prophet, saying, I will open my mouth in parables; I will utter things which have been kept secret from the foundation of the world.*[238]

"How do we find these secrets?" "As I said earlier, we compare the Old Testament text against the New Testament. So what takes place next?"

LINK 50: The Brethren Took Him

The pastor scanned the last verse of the account of Samson. *"The text says that his brethren and all the house of his father came down, and took him, and brought him up..."* "Do you see the correlation pastor?" "Yes, the description of the event is in all of the gospels. I like the connection in Luke." *And, behold, [there was] a man named Joseph, a counsellor; [and he was] a good man, and a just: ...And he took it down, and wrapped it in linen, and laid it in a sepulchre that was hewn in stone, wherein never man before was laid. ...And the women also, which came with him from Galilee, followed after, and beheld the sepulchre, and how his body was laid.*[239]

"Good observation pastor. Note that in both passages they took him. Also, if we read the other gospels we find that others

---

238 Matthew 13:34, 35.
239 Luke 23:50-55.

were involved. In John we find that Nicodemus[240] brought spices so that they could wrap the body." "And if I read the accounts of Matthew[241] and Mark[242] we find that His mother Mary and Mary the mother of Joses went with the procession to the tomb." "So you see pastor, it's very important that we compare the observations of all four gospel writers. Likewise, when we study the Old Testament accounts of the Guardians we must compare the passages with the gospel accounts."

LINK 51: Both were Buried

The pastor scanned the last few verses of the account of Samson in the Book of Judges and said, "Well they were both buried. Jesus was placed in the tomb and Samson was taken to be buried." "What specifically does the text say?"

Then his brethren and all the house of his father came down, and took him, and brought [him] up.[243]

"What do you hear or see?"

"Are you insinuating that Christ ascended to heaven with the entire household of His Father?" "It's as you say pastor but whether your understanding is right or not is immaterial. We'll soon arrive at the heart of the mystery that has evaded many." I replied with a smile. "Let's reconstruct the events following the resurrection using the four Gospels as our template."

"Pastor, according to my reading there were two Ascensions. The second Ascension took place after Jesus spent 40 days with His followers teaching them the unsealed messages. The first Ascension occurred on the first day of the week. And the first Ascension may have been one of the most important events since the Fall of man. The very day that Jesus had arisen from the grave

240 John 19:39.
241 Matthew 27:57-61.
242 Mark 15:43-47.
243 Judges 16:31.

He told Mary Magdalene not to touch Him because He had not yet ascended to His Father."

> *Jesus saith unto her, Mary. She turned herself, and saith unto him, Rabboni; which is to say, Master. Jesus saith unto her, <u>Touch me not</u>; for I am not yet ascended to my Father: but go to my brethren, and say unto them, I ascend unto my Father, and your Father; and [to] my God, and your God.*[244]

"Yet, next we see Jesus on the evening following the resurrection mysteriously appearing to two of the disciples on the road to Emmaus. Equally as mysterious, later that same day He appeared to the apostles and disciples in the Upper Room and invited them **to handle Him** and determine for themselves that He was not a ghost."

> *And, behold, two of them went that same day to a village called Emmaus, which was from Jerusalem [about] threescore furlongs. And they talked together of all these things which had happened. And it came to pass, that, while they communed [together] and reasoned, Jesus himself drew near, and went with them. And beginning at Moses and all the prophets, he expounded unto them in all the scriptures the things concerning himself... And they rose up the same hour, and returned to Jerusalem, and found the eleven gathered together, and them that were with them, Saying, The Lord is risen indeed, and hath appeared to Simon. And they told what things [were done] in the way, and how he was known of them in breaking of bread. And as they thus spake, Jesus himself stood in the midst of them, and saith unto them, Peace [be] unto you. But they were terrified and affrighted, and supposed that they had seen a spirit. And he said unto them, Why are ye troubled? and why do thoughts arise in your hearts? Behold my hands and my feet, that it is I*

---

244 John 20:16, 17.

myself: <u>handle me, and see; for a spirit hath not flesh and bones, as ye see me have.</u>[245]

"Pastor, Jesus ascended to His Father between the time He left Mary Magdalene at the tomb and the time He was seen on the road to Emmaus. Similarly, Samson was taken up to be by his father."

"But where do we find the details on His ascension? And why is this event so important?"

"Turn with me to the fifth chapter of the Book of Revelation of Jesus Christ and listen very carefully to the words. The text says:

And I saw in the right hand of him that sat on the throne a book written within and on the backside, sealed with seven seals. And I saw a strong angel proclaiming with a loud voice, Who is worthy to open the book, and to loose the seals thereof? And no man in heaven, nor in earth, neither under the earth, was able to open the book, neither to look thereon. And I [John] wept much, because no man was found worthy to open and to read the book, neither to look thereon. And one of the elders saith unto me, Weep not: behold, the Lion of the tribe of Juda, the Root of David, hath prevailed to open the book, and to loose the seven seals thereof. And I beheld, and, lo, in the midst of the throne and of the four beasts, and in the midst of the elders, <u>stood a Lamb as it had been slain, having seven horns and seven eyes, which are the seven Spirits of God sent forth into all the earth.</u> And he came and took the book out of the right hand of him that sat upon the throne. And when he had taken the book, the four beasts and four [and] twenty elders fell down before the Lamb, having every one of them harps, and golden vials full of odours, which are the prayers of saints. And they sung a new song, saying, Thou art worthy to take the book, and to open the seals thereof: for thou wast slain, and hast redeemed us to God by thy blood out of every

---

245 Luke 24:13-15, 27, 33-38.

kindred, and tongue, and people, and nation; And hast made us unto our God kings and priests: and we shall reign on the earth. And I beheld, and I heard the voice of many angels round about the throne and the beasts and the elders: and the number of them was ten thousand times ten thousand, and thousands of thousands; Saying with a loud voice, Worthy is the Lamb that was slain to receive power, and riches, and wisdom, and strength, and honour, and glory, and blessing.[246]

"What's the sealed book?" he asked. "It's the key to the mysteries and secrets but we'll get to that in a few moments," I replied. "But most importantly, the Lamb was found to be worthy to open it. If He had not been found worthy, the entire Plan of Salvation would have been a failure. But, He was found worthy."

Emmaus Experience: Revelations of Christ

"Pastor, turn with me again to the passage we read a moment ago in the twenty fourth chapter of Luke."

And, behold, two of them went that same day to a village called Emmaus, which was from Jerusalem [about] threescore furlongs. And they talked together of all these things which had happened. And it came to pass, that, while they communed [together] and reasoned, Jesus himself drew near, and went with them. But their eyes were holden that they should not know him. And he said unto them, What manner of communications [are] these that ye have one to another, as ye walk, and are sad? And the one of them, whose name was Cleopas, answering said unto him, Art thou only a stranger in Jerusalem, and hast not known the things which are come to pass there in these days? And he said unto them,

---

246 Revelation 5:1-12.

What things? And they said unto him, Concerning Jesus of Nazareth, which was a prophet mighty in deed and word before God and all the people:

And how the chief priests and our rulers delivered him to be condemned to death, and have crucified him. But we trusted that it had been he which should have redeemed Israel: and beside all this, to day is the third day since these things were done. Yea, and certain women also of our company made us astonished, which were early at the sepulchre; And when they found not his body, they came, saying, that they had also seen a vision of angels, which said that he was alive. And certain of them which were with us went to the sepulchre, and found [it] even so as the women had said: but him they saw not. <u>Then he said unto them, O fools, and slow of heart to believe all that the prophets have spoken: Ought not Christ to have suffered these things, and to enter into his glory? And beginning at Moses and all the prophets, he expounded unto them in all the scriptures the things concerning himself.</u> And their eyes were opened, and they knew him; and he vanished out of their sight.[247]

"Did you hear that pastor? The moment the Jesus returned to Earth in human form, He tells the disciples on the Road to Emmaus that the writings of Moses and all the prophets are all about Himself! Jesus immediately began opening the secret hidden treasures of the Old Testament to them. And these treasures were the hidden testimonies of a great cloud of witnesses proclaiming that Jesus Christ is Lord. He also revealed the Plan of Salvation that was hid in plain sight. There was no further need to keep the Plan of Salvation a secret because all had been fulfilled. Now that the victory had been won and the House of Dagon, or should I say the House of Satan, had been destroyed neither man nor Satan could thwart His Plan."

"What does this have to do with the seven sealed Book?"

---

247 Luke 24:13-27, 31.

Unlocking the 7 Sealed Book

"The seven sealed Book had been locked until the Lamb slain from the foundation of the World, the Lion of the Tribe of Judah, Jesus Christ had been crucified. It couldn't be unlocked until a worthy Being could be found to open it. And that worthy one was Jesus, the Lamb slain from the foundation of the world. The writings within the Sealed Book contain the mysteries that were hidden so that the Plan of Salvation could be completed." The Scriptures say:

> *we speak the wisdom of God in a mystery, [even] the hidden [wisdom], which God ordained before the world unto our glory: Which none of the princes of this world knew: for had they known [it], they would not have crucified the Lord of glory.*[248]

"When Christ had completed His mission, the Old Testament Scriptures were opened. Think about it. The angels around the throne of God cried because no one was worthy to open the Book. But when Jesus approached the Hand of the One that held the Book, the angels recognized that the Lamb slain from the Foundation of the world was worthy to open the Book. The Book that was handed to the Lamb with the Seven Seals was the entirety of the Scriptures woven into the Book of Revelation. So the vision that was later given to John on the Isle of Patmos was intertwined with every book of the Old Testament." "What's in this Unsealed Book?" "The Unsealed Book is written on a roll that records the history of God's protection and spiritual care for His people from the time of Adam to the end of time. It records in symbolic language the walk of God with His people, the Church, the rise and fall of kingdoms and the destiny of every nation, kindred, and tongue."

"How do we know that this scene took place right after the resurrection?"

---

248 1 Corinthians 2:7,8.

LAMB WITH 7 HORNS AND 7 EYES: Horns are symbols of power, eyes are symbols of seeing, and 7 is a symbol of completeness. The little lamb that came to the throne with 7 horns and 7 eyes is all powerful and all knowing. He is the omnipotent and omniscient Lamb of God: Jesus Christ. Most importantly, He is the only one worthy to open the seven sealed book.

"You might say that until the resurrection Christ was concealed in the Old Testament. But once He met His disciples on the Road to Emmaus we see Jesus revealed. You might say that *the Old*

Testament and the New Testaments are both Revelations of Jesus Christ. What is found in symbols in the Book of Revelation connects with events in the Old Testament. The Old Testament, the Gospels, the New Testament, and the Book of Revelation are all like pieces of our treasure map. When the pieces of the map are assembled they give the complete view of the Plan. That is, they plainly reveal the Plan of Salvation and demonstrate that Jesus Christ was with His people from the beginning."[249] "And so, with His victory over Satan and death, Jesus returned to earth and met the two disciples on their way to Emmaus. It was then that He began to open the Old Testament to His disciples and His apostles."

Upper Room Awakening

"After Jesus had walked with His disciples on the road to Emmaus, He went to tell the Good News to the apostles and disciples in the Upper Room in Jerusalem. Imagine the shock that frightened the apostles and disciples when Jesus entered the Upper Room. They were hiding, fearing for their lives and having lost hope that Jesus was the Messiah."

And as they thus spake, Jesus himself stood in the midst of them, and saith unto them, Peace [be] unto you. But <u>they were terrified and affrighted</u>, and supposed that they had seen a spirit. And he said unto them, Why are ye troubled? and why do thoughts arise in your hearts? Behold my hands and my feet, that it is I myself: handle me, and see; for a spirit hath not flesh and bones, as ye see me have. And when he had thus spoken, he showed them [his] hands and [his] feet. And while they yet believed not for joy, and wondered, he said unto them, Have ye here any meat? And they gave him a piece of a broiled fish, and of an honeycomb. And he took [it], and did eat before them. And he said unto them, These [are] the words which I spake unto you, while I was yet with

---

249 1 Corinthians 10:4.

you, that all things must be fulfilled, <u>which were written</u> <u>in the law of Moses, and [in] the prophets, and [in] the</u> <u>psalms, concerning me.</u>   <u>Then opened he their</u> <u>understanding, that they might understand the scriptures,</u> And said unto them, Thus it is written, and thus it behoved Christ to suffer, and to rise from the dead the third day: And that repentance and remission of sins should be preached in his name among all nations, beginning at Jerusalem. And ye are witnesses of these things.[250]

"Notice that it was then that He opened their understanding that they might understand the secrets and mysteries of the Old Testament. Again, Jesus opened the Scriptures, explaining to them how all the writings of Moses, and the psalmists, and the prophets were about Him. During the 40 days after His appearance in the Upper Room, Jesus pointed to the evidence that He is the Christ. Based on these experiences all but one of the apostles were willing to die to share the message. All were murdered except John and even John was put in a boiling pot of oil. All 12 apostles were absolutely convinced that He was the Messiah."

Open Book

After His resurrection:

Jesus began both to do and teach, Until the day in which <u>he was taken up</u>, <u>after that </u>he through the Holy Ghost had given commandments unto the apostles whom he had chosen: To whom also <u>he showed himself alive after his</u> <u>passion by many infallible proofs, being seen of them</u> <u> forty days</u>, and speaking of the things pertaining to the kingdom of God.[251]

"Jesus spent the forty days with His disciples teaching the most incredible Bible study of all time. He proved to them that the

---

250 Luke 24:36-48.
251 Acts 1:1-3.

Scriptures were all about Himself. He showed them that all the symbols, shadows, and types behind the characters of the Old Testament, behind the Levitical feasts, in the writings of Moses, the prophets, and the psalms, and in the sanctuary pointed to Jesus and His Plan of Salvation. It was the Revelation of Jesus Christ. All this happened before his Ascension." "I wish I'd been there for that bible study." "Me too pastor."

"In its entirety, the Old Testament provides, in meticulous detail, the war between Christ and Satan. The detail is provided in such a way that the reader has to spend time putting the pieces of the puzzle together. He wants you to spend time with Him."

"And Jesus is now the one that holds the keys to the kingdom."

> *I [am] he that liveth, and was dead; and, behold, I am alive for evermore, Amen; and have the keys of hell and of death.*[252]

"Jesus had been granted power over hell and death in His first ascension." "How can you say that?" "We're told that as Jesus gave his followers the Great Commission on the Mount of Olives He also told them that He had been given all power in heaven and earth."

> *And Jesus came and spake unto them, saying, All power is given unto me in heaven and in earth. Go ye therefore, and teach all nations, baptizing them in the name of the Father, and of the Son, and of the Holy Ghost.*[253]

"His power was given to Him before His second ascension from the Mount of Olives. He had already been given ALL POWER and the permission to expose the Plan of Salvation because He and He alone had been found worthy to open the Book. So upon His return on the Road to Emmaus He began to open it up. And He explained it to the apostles in the Upper Room and for the following forty days. And He now offers those same keys to you

---

252 Revelation 1:18.
253 Matthew 28:18, 19.

and me. If you spend time in the unsealed Book, you'll find divine treasures through the study of the types and prophecies that will strengthen your faith.   You'll read the testimonies of a great cloud of witnesses, just like Samson, professing that Jesus Christ is Lord." "You might say that the seven sealed Book was opened before the Book of Revelation was penned by John on the island of Patmos. For the Revelation of Jesus Christ is found both in the Old and New Testaments."

LINK 52: Judges Israel

"Until the Synagogue of Satan, was destroyed and Jesus' sacrifice was found to be worthy, the Plan of Salvation was shrouded behind a veil. Likewise, Jesus came to Planet Earth shrouded in a veil of human flesh. When the Plan of Salvation had been fulfilled, the veil that hid the way to the Holiest Place was torn from top to bottom; the veil that hid Jesus and His Plan of Salvation in the Old Testament was pulled away; and the flesh that cloaked Jesus with humanity was torn away and the Divinity of Jesus was revealed. The opening of the veil to the Holy place, the Revelation of Jesus behind the veil of the Scriptures, exposing His divinity in Gethsemane, and the tearing of His flesh all testify of and verify that Jesus Christ is the Son of God and that His Holy Scriptures are supernatural."

> *By a new and living way, which he hath consecrated for us, through the veil, that is to say, his flesh; And [having] an high priest over the house of God.*[254]

"Jesus was cloaked by human flesh while He dwelt among us."

> *Forasmuch then as the children are partakers of flesh and blood, he also himself likewise took part of the same; that through death he might destroy him that had the power of death, that is, the devil; And deliver them who through fear of death were all their lifetime subject to*

---

254 Hebrews 10:20,21.

bondage. For verily he took not on [him the nature of] angels; but he took on [him] the seed of Abraham. Wherefore in all things it behoved him to be made like unto [his] brethren, that he might be a merciful and faithful high priest in things [pertaining] to God, to make reconciliation for the sins of the people. For in that he himself hath suffered being tempted, he is able to succour them that are tempted.[255]

"Christ's death on the Cross gave Him power over death and leads to the destruction of Satan. Jesus was exposed to the sins of the world just like any other man. Through His exceedingly painful and sorrowful experience, Jesus can identify with our trials and tribulations. He paid the price for our freedom, and He now sits as the judge of our destiny." Therefore:

Fear God, and give glory to him; for the hour of his judgment is come: and worship him that made heaven, and earth, and the sea, and the fountains of waters.[256]

"The Jews sought to kill Jesus not only because He had broken the traditions of the elders on how to keep the Sabbath[257] but because He also said that God was His Father, making Himself equal with God. In response to their murderous intentions, Jesus responded saying the Father hath committed all judgment unto the Son."

For as the Father raiseth up the dead, and quickeneth [them]; even so the Son quickeneth whom he will. For the Father judgeth no man, but hath committed all judgment unto the Son: That all [men] should honour the Son[258]

---

255 Hebrews 2:14-18.
256 Revelation 14:7.
257 Matthew 15:1-7; Mark 7:7-13.
258 John 5:21-23.

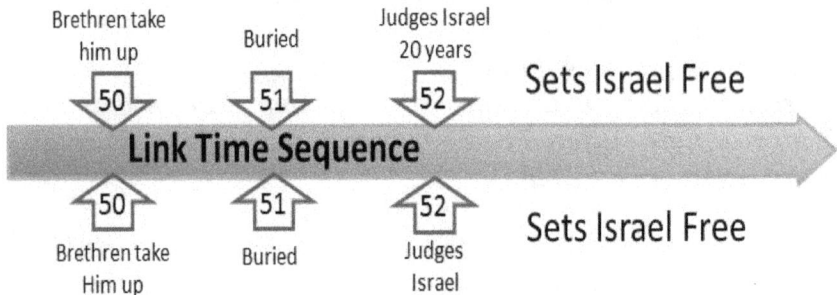

Summary of Event Connections

The tables provide the summary of the 52 connections between the accounts of Samson and Jesus. The account of Samson is recorded as 96 verses in the Book of Judges approximately 1100 years before the birth of Christ. Based on these results and others yet to be shared, it is clear that the connections between Samson and Jesus are not coincidence. Rather, it is clear that the connections are deliberate. Only some Being or Beings with the ability to know future events far in advance could have embedded the code for future generations to discover. The most striking realization is that these 52 events and others not included in our analyses are in the same temporal sequence.

Could it be that Jesus is the Messiah, just as He claims? Could it be that God exists? Could it be that the writings of the Bible and the embedded code were guided by some unseen Holy Spirit? As intriguing as this is, the books to follow in this series provide even more profound evidence of the existence of the supernatural. And each of the Guardians make a Great Cloud of Witnesses.

How else can you explain the following connections between Samson and Jesus:

1. Eight links connect their miracle births in parallel order;
2. They both are driven by the Holy Spirit and defeat the roaring lion;
3. Both provide a riddle about a change of garments;
4. One sets the fields on fire and the other sets the world on fire; both send them out two by two;
5. One physically kills thousands with a jawbone while the other kills the old man and brings newness of life by jawboning (preaching). Afterwards both end speaking;
6. Plots are made to kill them both but the gates of hell cannot contain them;
7. Both are sold for silver;
8. Both are captured, blinded (or blindfolded), bound and imprisoned. Both had power from the 7 on their heads. One is powerful; the other is all powerful or omnipotent;
9. One is a great sacrifice. The other was the greatest sacrifice;
10. In their sacrifice both gained victory over the false god;
11. Both were taken up by their brethren; and
12. One judged Israel for twenty years and the other judges Israel to this very day.

Testimony of Samson

He was born when Israel was in captivity
His was a *MIRACLE BIRTH*
His **BIRTH WAS ANNOUNCED BY AN ANGEL FIRST TO HIS MOTHER AND THEN TO HIS FATHER**
He was Holy and set apart; Nazarite
the *DELIVERER OF ISRAEL*
His name means *"LIKE THE SUN"*
DRIVEN INTO THE WILDERNESS BY THE SPIRIT
HE SOUGHT THE BRIDE; HE WAS TEMPTED;
HE CONFRONTS THE ENEMY
and *HE SLAYS THE ROARING LION;*
Honey is the WORD in the One that was slain;
THEY SEND OUT THE WEDDING INVITATION;
He attends the *WEDDING;*
He gives the parable of the *CHANGE OF GARMENTS WHICH IS A SYMBOL OF REBIRTH*
Friend of the *BRIDEGROOM*
He *SENDS THEM OUT TWO BY TWO;*
THE FIREBRAND IS THE HOLY SPIRIT;
THEY SET THE WORLD ON FIRE
He uses the JAWBONE a SYMBOL of Preaching
He uses the Jawbone to slay them hip and thigh, a symbol of rebirth
He gains the *VICTORY OVER THOUSANDS ON TWO SEPARATE OCCASIONS*
HE RESTS IN A MOUNTAIN REFUGE BETWEEN THE TWO BATTLES
He makes an *END OF SPEAKING*

Testimony of Samson

The enemy attacks even more fiercely;
They PLOT TO KILL HIM
The GATES CANNOT HOLD Samson;
The GATES OF HELL CANNOT PREVAIL;
GATE IS SYMBOL OF THE DOOR TO THE TOMB;
He CARRIES THE GATE TO THE TOP OF HILL;
The HILL IS THE SYMBOL OF CALVARY
THE WOMAN IS A SYMBOL OF THE CHURCH
SOLD OUT FOR SILVER
BY DELILAH, THE CHURCH
HIS SOUL IS VEXED UNTO DEATH
HE IS LED LIKE A LAMB TO THE SLAUGHTER
7 LOCKS POINT TO THE 7 HORNS OF CHRIST
A HORN IS A SYMBOL OF POWER
7 IS A SYMBOL OF COMPLETENESS
HE IS ALL POWERFUL OR OMNIPOTENT
He is **BLINDED**; He is **BOUND**; He is **IMPRISONED**
His **CAPTORS REJOICE**; He is a *GREAT SACRIFICE*
DAGON IS A SYMBOL OF SATAN THE FALSE GOD;
They make sport of him;
HIS ARMS ARE OUTSTRETCHED
He **calls upon the Lord for strength**
He **DESTROYS THE TWO PILLARS OF SATAN:**
SIN AND DEATH;
DESTROYS THE HOUSE OF DAGON
SLEW MORE IN DEATH THAN IN LIFE
Taken up by His Brethren and Buried;
JUDGES ISRAEL

15 *Harmony of Types*

And what shall I more say? for the time would fail me to tell of Gedeon, and [of] Barak, and [of] Samson, and [of] Jephthae; [of] David also, and Samuel, and [of] the prophets:[259] *Wherefore seeing we also are compassed about with so great a cloud of witnesses, let us lay aside every weight, and the sin which doth so easily beset [us], and let us run with patience the race that is set before us...*[260]

Unlocking the account of Samson is just the beginning of our journey. "Pastor, the Bible is much, much more than a book." "I would agree. But explain to me what you're driving at." "It's a supernatural treasure map of past, present, and future events. And it's filled with witnesses bearing clues. When you begin to decipher the text you find messages concealed as cyphers within cyphers like wheels within wheels; each one fitting together in precision.[261] I view it as a multifaceted cryptogram in which each clue adds more and more clarity about the events in the earthly walk of Jesus hundreds of years before His birth. And the Cross is at the center of the cryptogram." "Why do you believe God made sure that there are multiple witnesses?" "Multiple witnesses make an iron clad case."

"The evidence confirms that a supernatural Being or Beings have guided the writing of the Scriptures while deliberately hiding evidence that would be opened at the right time." "Why the concern about hiding the evidence?" "Like I said earlier, if the powers of the world had known they wouldn't have crucified Christ and without the crucifixion the rescue Plan would have failed." "So the evidence was scattered behind the accounts of numerous Guardians throughout the Old Testament?"

---

259 Hebrews 11:32.
260 Hebrews 12:1, 2.
261 Ezekiel 1:16.

"Deliberately! Selected connections were hidden among a large number of Old Testament characters like Samson. It's as if the treasure map was divided into many smaller pieces and hidden throughout the writings. Selected is the key word. By using this approach, it's apparent that the Being or Beings made the connections to Christ look coincidental when the Scriptures are studied superficially. But they become evident when you begin to unlock the hidden messages."

Harmony of Old Testament Types

The pastor had a puzzled look on his face. "Pastor, like we discussed earlier today, each of our Guardians holds only a portion of the map or keys to open selected events in the earthly walk of Jesus. No Guardian holds all the keys." "Then how are your findings any different than the findings and analyses of theologians that study types?"

"The significant discovery is that there's a **Harmony of the deciphered accounts of Old Testament types of Christ** just as theologians have long known that there's a **Harmony of the Gospels.** When each of the pieces of the puzzle are put together the full view of the Plan of Salvation is revealed." "I get it. That's powerful." "Very powerful. The New Testament displays harmony among physical events found within the testimony of the four Gospels. By comparison, the events in the accounts of the types of Jesus in the Old Testament Scriptures have to be deciphered because they're cast in a spiritual context. So the New Testament exhibits physical harmony and the Old Testament exhibits spiritual harmony." "So how do you apply it?" "Once you understand the concept, you can use the knowledge to align the physical events of the New with the spiritual meanings of the Old. That's why I use the event sequence in the New Testament as a template to unlock the spiritual significance of events in the Old." "What else have you learned from your studies?"

"As I see it, there are two fundamental conclusions. First, the account of each Old Testament witness provides a unique portion of the puzzle just like Matthew, Mark, Luke, and John do in the New Testament. When these unique accounts are assembled we see a more complete picture of the earthly walk of Christ. The power in the evidence being provided by the Supernatural Author is that the testimony of multiple witnesses proves the case for the existence of God. The scripture says, *take with thee one or two more, that in the mouth of two or three witnesses every word may be established.*"[262]

"So God is building an evidentiary based case?"

"Yes! He's building the case for those that willingly search the Scriptures and seek to find Him. The collective evidence proves that He exists and that His Word is Truth."

"So you're convinced that God is working through multiple witnesses to provide us the evidence we need to believe in Him?"

"Without a doubt, pastor. I'm absolutely convinced that each character, or type of Christ, holds a single piece of a larger puzzle. The events in the lives of each of our witnesses are deliberately selected or you could say they're supernaturally guided to give us complementary insights into the Being we call Jesus. The more clues we unearth the better we understand the Plan to rescue mankind. For example, both Samson and Jesus were driven by the Holy Spirit to confront the enemy at the same point in their lives. That wasn't by coincidence. One was a physical enemy and the other was a supernatural enemy. To me, you might say each witness gives us glimpses of different events in the life of Christ."

"Samson's testimony seems to provide more than an overwhelming iron clad case to me. What more do you need to make the case that Jesus is the Messiah and that God exists?"

"I agree, but even though Samson's testimony alone is amazing and compelling, there are a Great Cloud of Witnesses that make the case unassailable. You might want to disagree about my interpretation of some of the events in the life of Samson but the

---

262 Matthew 18:16.

ties between the pillars or major events are clear. And when you consider the case of Samson with the testimonies of a great number of other witnesses the case becomes certain." "Why was it so important that there be a great cloud of witnesses?"

"God's character is being attacked by Satan through numerous avenues. To this very day Satan is working through unbelievers who are scoffing at the writing of the Scriptures. Knowing this in advance, God in His great wisdom, provides hidden evidence of the Plan to rescue mankind in the accounts of His witnesses throughout the Old Testament for such a time as this. Those that seek the Truth will find it."

"I'm beginning to understand why Samson's included as a witness in the "Faith" chapter of the Book of Hebrews. In the end he had the faith to trust in God and in the end he saved Israel from bondage by bringing down the house of Dagon just as Jesus brought down the house of Satan. If you hadn't made the connection between Jesus and Samson I wouldn't have pictured Samson as a type of Christ. The unlocked account of Samson provides an unquestionable type of Christ. From the Divine announcement of their births, to the supernatural spirit driven confrontation with the lion, to the plots to trap and murder them, being sold out for silver, being bound, imprisoned, blinded, even dying with their arms outstretched to destroy their enemies, there's no question that there's an uncanny supernatural connection between them, and that connection had to be deliberate."

"I couldn't agree more!" "Could you give me examples of how other underlying testimonies complement Samson's testimony?" "I can give you lots of examples but we don't have time to do an in-depth study. We're almost at your stop. Select a couple of types of Christ that you've studied and I'll show you how they complement Samson's testimony." "How about Isaac and Jonah. Christ himself pointed to the account of Jonah as a type of Christ's own death burial and resurrection. Why don't we start there?" Within a few minutes the pastor and I could see the principle of the Harmony of the Old Testament types. We could plainly see that the events in the account of Isaac filled in ties to events found in the account of Jesus not found in the account of Samson.

Jesus	Samson	Isaac	Jonah
Sold for silver	Sold for silver		
Blindfolded	Blinded		
Bound	Bound		
Imprisoned	Imprisoned		
Make fun of Him	Make fun of him		
Carries wood for sacrifice to Calvary (same as Moriah)		Carries wood for sacrifice to top of hill Moriah	
Dies with arms outstretched	Dies with arms outstretched		
Crown of thorns		Crown of thorns	
Lamb of God as substitute		Ram provided by God as substitute	
Blood sacrifice substitute		Blood sacrifice substitute	
Destroys house of false god (Satan)	Destroys house of false god (Dagon)		
In belly of the earth			In belly of hell "Hell" is defined as the grave
Son resurrected on third day			Vomited (resurrected) on the third day

HARMONY OF OLD TESTAMENT TYPES The table illustrates how deciphered events of several Old Testament characters provide complementary evidence that God exists.

The Old Testament characters each hide their own unique keys for unlocking the Scriptures. You might say each holds parts of the treasure map. No two pieces are alike. As illustrated in the table above, deciphered events in the accounts of Isaac, Jonah, and Samson provide a more in-depth look at the events of the earthly walk of Jesus than recorded in the Gospels alone.

"Imagine how much evidence resides in the Guardians from Genesis to Malachi, from Adam to Zerubbabel, from A to Z. After all, there are over two thousand names in the Scriptures that carry meaning." The following are just a small handful of our Guardians of the Code:

Aaron: a figure of Christ as High Priest
Abraham: God the Father
Boaz: Christ our Kinsman Redeemer
Cyrus: Christ the Deliverer of Israel from Babylon
Daniel: Christ raised from the "lion's" tomb
David: Christ the King of Kings
Elisha: Christ the miracle worker
Isaac: Christ our Sacrifice
Israel: Christ our Overcomer of Sin
Jonah: Christ Resurrected from the Tomb
Joseph: "Savior of the World" [name]
Joshua: "Yahweh is Salvation" [name]
Melchizedek: Christ, "King of Righteousness" [name]
Mordecai: Christ the Warrior [name] on the White Horse
Moses: Christ the Lawgiver and Deliverer
Noah: Christ our "Comforter" [name]
Passover Lamb: Christ our Sacrifice
Samson: Christ the All-Powerful or Omnipotent
Seed of the Woman: Christ He will crush the serpent
Solomon: Christ the All-Wise (Omniscient) Prince of Peace
Zerubbabel: Christ the One that sets the Foundation

"Bible names deliberately carry depth of meaning. Some describe revelations of God's purposes, some provide clues to unlocking an account, and still other names like *"Methuselah"* meaning *"his death shall bring (the flood)"* convey prophecies of the future. When Methuselah died the Flood came as the fulfillment of the prophecy in his name! Each name should be carefully examined because many provide clues and convey information key to the account. For example Jacob's name was changed to *"Israel"* which means *"overcomer"* of sin. And we all want to overcome sin and become members of Spiritual Israel."

"The Old Testament testimonies provide revelations of unexplored dimensions yet they remain largely untapped by mankind. And yet their collective evidence illuminates the Cross and provides detailed information about end time events and the Second Coming of Christ. Why wouldn't we want to tap into the evidence? The destiny of mankind may depend upon it."

"When you assemble the pieces of a puzzle you see a picture. Likewise, when you put the keys together a beautiful vision of the Plan of Salvation comes into view, the likes of which few have ever seen or understood." "So what's the next step?"

"We piece their deciphered information together just like we did in our table." Nodding his head he replied, "I get it! Say, what about the account of Jonah. There must be more ties within the account of Jonah."

I grinned and said, "You don't know how right you are. I've been working on the treasures of Jonah and I'll soon publish a book on it. When I complete the book I'll send you a copy."

16 *Unexplored Dimensions of the Cross*

For Christ sent me not to baptize, but to preach the gospel: not with wisdom of words, lest the cross of Christ should be made of none effect. For the preaching of the cross is to them that perish foolishness; but unto us which are saved it is the <u>power</u> of God.[263]

We were traveling through the majestic mountain passes of Glacier National Park at dusk just as the sun set over the mountains. I always look upon the setting sun as a metaphor of Christ dying upon the Cross. Even though we talked all day, neither of us was weary of talking about the Scriptures. Each scene in the account of Christ and His Plan to rescue mankind can be understood in far greater depth by assembling and comparing portions of the treasure map held by several Guardians.

"Can you give me an example of how the individual characters give a richer view of a special event in the life of Christ?" "I'd be happy to give you an example. As we decipher each Guardian's hidden portion of the code, we can assemble them together like you would a puzzle or treasure map. Just looking at our table, you can see that there's a lot of information surrounding the events of the Cross." The pastor smiled nodding in agreement. "We don't have time to fully explore the dimensions of the Cross but I can give you examples of how to unlock its deeper meanings." "That would be great!"

"When you put several deciphered portions of the Old Testament Cross together with the physical account of the Cross, a beautiful vision comes into view, the likes of which few have ever seen or

---

[263] 1 Corinthians 1:17, 18.

understood. By taking our approach, we can get an idea of the emotional trauma suffered by God the Father and we can see Satan claiming victory only to have the tables turned. It adds to the depth of drama and imagery that we don't see in the reading of the Gospel accounts alone." Nodding his head he replied, "I get it!"

House of Satan Destroyed

"Let's use Samson to illustrate how piecing the deciphered events provide more understanding of the events at the Cross. When Samson spread out his arms and caused the pillars of Dagon to crumble it symbolized the destruction of the House of Satan and the toppling of the pillars of sin and death. Where do you get that information in the Gospels? You don't. When Christ died, He overcame sin and death. That's why the graves were opened and the veil of the temple was torn. No longer would humanity need the sacrificial service." "What a rescue Plan!"

"When I study the Cross and consider it from the perspective of the message of Samson I see the Cross at the very intersection of time and space. I see the epicenter of healing shooting out through the time space continuum like the waves of a tsunami. As Samson stretched out his arms, Christ likewise stretched out His. Samson put his hands on two pillars and brought down the House of Dagon. Likewise, Jesus destroyed the pillars of sin and death and destroyed the House of Satan."

"I see how the Cross has impacted lives after the death of Christ but how do you draw the conclusion that this supernatural tsunami heals those that died in the past?"

Time-Space Epicenter of Healing

"We have to turn to another Guardian of the Code to understand that the impact of the Cross also heals those with faith throughout recorded history all the way back to Adam. You could say that the shock wave travelled out from the epicenter of the Cross in all directions. If you study the account of our Guardian Joshua, you'll see that when Christ crossed over the Jordan, or should I say the Ark of the Testimony crossed over the Jordan, the cleansing waters of the Jordan rolled back all the way to a place called Adam." "Wow! Could you show me?"

"If we look at the passage in Joshua you'll understand."

That the waters which came down from above stood [and] rose up upon an heap very far from the city <u>Adam</u>, that [is] beside Zaretan: and those that came down toward the sea of the plain, [even] the salt sea, failed, [and] were cut off: and the people passed over right against Jericho.[264]

"What does the passage tell us?" "Metaphorically, the healing waters of the Jordan washed away the sins of mankind all the way back to Adam and carried away the sins of the world. And the words *cut off* refer to the cutting off of the life of Jesus. When you consider that the wages of sin is **death** you realize that the passage also tells us that our sins are carried away by supernatural cleansing waters to a place called the **Dead** Sea."

"Beautiful. Is there more?" I nodded and continued, "Yes, you see the people of Israel passed over Jordan in front of the Ark of the Testimony. You might say that each of us that overcomes sin and death must pass before the Ark so that our sins may be washed away by the blood of Jesus. The cleansing of our sins is represented by the Day of Atonement Feast that took place in the sanctuary. And it was all because of Christ's sacrifice."

And the LORD said unto Joshua, This day have I rolled away the reproach of Egypt from off you. Wherefore the name of the place is called Gilgal unto this day.[265]

"You see, when we as the people of God Cross over the Jordan our sins are metaphorically washed away. The sins that we pick up in Egypt, a metaphor for the world of sin, are washed away at the

---

264 Joshua 3:16.
265 Joshua 5:9.

Crossing of Jordan near a place appropriately called Gilgal. Amazingly, **Gilgal in Hebrew is the same as Golgotha in Syriac**. We come to the foot of the Cross and we come before the Ark to cleanse ourselves of sin. So you see, when we look at this instance in Joshua together with the account of Samson we see that the blood of Jesus was like a healing wave that emanated throughout time past and time future rolling back the reproach of Egypt, or should I say the sins of mankind. Each Guardian adds a unique perspective. If you study the accounts of Joseph, Daniel, David and numerous other Guardians, the Cross becomes a study of epic proportions. It's at the epicenter of history and the most profound event in the history of mankind. Without it, we'd all be doomed to eternal death."

"Professor, God truly took us through a secret passageway. Yet I've studied the Scriptures for decades and I've never taken the trip through this passageway before. Now, more than ever I understand what Jesus said to John:"

> **Behold, I stand at the door, and knock: if any man hear my voice, and open the door, I will come in to him, and will sup with him, and he with me.**[266]

"Pastor, my conclusion is that the Bible is an infinite Book. It's an intersection between two universes. It's a bridge or ladder between the eternal world of heaven and the physical world of planet Earth. It points to our eternal home; a place that has no beginning and no end. After all, God is Eternal and without end. So is His Word. We'll never be able to digest it all."

A Father's Love

"Let me give you another insight about the Cross. Pastor, do you have a son?" "Yes!" "Consider how you might feel if you were directed by God to kill your son with a knife as if you were sacrificing a lamb at the temple." The pastor shuddered and said,

---

266 Revelation 3:20.

"I don't see how I could go through with it. I'd rather take my own life." "That very image is used to give us a feeling for how God the Father felt as He watched His Son on the Cross. We can only imagine how God the Father felt as each swing of the hammer drove the spikes through Christ's hands and feet; the Father must have shuddered in agony. God could have stopped the pain. But God so loved the world that He gave His Son that we might be saved. It had to be unbearable. That's the picture that the figure of Abraham and Isaac gives us. It was as if Abraham, acting in the part of God the Father, was being tried in the fire."

> **By faith Abraham, when he was tried, offered up Isaac: and he that had received the promises offered up his only begotten [son]. Of whom it was said, That in Isaac shall thy seed be called: Accounting that God [was] able to raise [him] up, even from the dead; from whence also he received him in a figure.**[267]

"But why would a loving God put Abraham through such stress?" "God was testing his faith. And Abraham had faith. He was convinced that if his son were sacrificed, God would raise him from the dead because Isaac was key to the Promise made to Abraham. It's the kind of faith God wants each of us to have. In the end, God provided Isaac with a substitute. He provided a lamb wearing a crown of thorns as a symbol that pointed to Jesus. Likewise, God has provided each of us with Jesus as our Lamb wearing a crown of thorns if we would just believe. If the Pharisees understood the Akedah or *"**Binding of Isaac**,"* they would have immediately drawn the parallel when the Romans placed a crown of thorns on the head of Jesus." "Maybe they did."

Battle at the Cross

"The New Testament doesn't give us much understanding about the supernatural events taking place around the Cross. The real war was unseen to mortal eyes. Satan was doing everything he

---

267 Hebrews 11:17-19.

could to cause Christ to reveal himself and step down from the Cross. But if Christ stepped down, the Plan of Salvation would have failed. Satan was using underhanded tactics just like he had in the wilderness temptation of Christ. But Satan added a new twist. Satan spoke through the people to provoke Jesus to make a misstep. It's excruciatingly hurtful to have your friends turn against you. Imagine if you heard the words of Satan coming through those that once loved you. Since Jesus cared deeply about the destiny of His followers He must've grieved terribly at how some of His followers treated Him even though He knew Satan's angels were prompting them. Even the Pharisees unwittingly tempted Him to step down off the Cross."

And they that passed by reviled him, wagging their heads, And saying, Thou that destroyest the temple, and buildest [it] in three days, save thyself. If thou be the Son of God, come down from the cross.[268]

"Professor, I agree with you that the demons possessed those that opposed Christ in the crowd and through their hosts taunted Him to come down off the Cross were the same that screamed out "Crucify Him! Crucify Him!"[269] "Without a doubt. Christ was all alone in the battle just as He was in the wilderness temptation. He had to win out of love. Had He stepped off the Cross, the hidden Plan would have failed." "It's no wonder Christ said, *Father, forgive them; for they know not what they do*. They really didn't know what they were doing. Their thoughts had been taken over by demons."[270]

"Imagine being surrounded with such wickedness and being all alone. He was like the Lamb led to the slaughter. Perhaps the two best descriptions of how Jesus felt in His last few moments are recorded in Isaiah 53 and Psalms 22." "I know those chapters very well, Professor." He pointed to Psalm 22:

---

268 Matthew 27:39, 40.
269 Luke 23:21.
270 Luke 23:34.

They gaped upon me [with] their mouths, [as] a ravening and a roaring lion. I am poured out like water, and all my bones are out of joint: my heart is like wax; it is melted in the midst of my bowels. My strength is dried up like a potsherd; and my tongue cleaveth to my jaws; and thou hast brought me into the dust of death. For dogs have compassed me: the assembly of the wicked have enclosed me: <u>they pierced my hands and my feet</u>. I may tell all my bones: they look [and] stare upon me. <u>They part my garments among them, and cast lots upon my vesture</u>. But be not thou far from me, O LORD: O my strength, haste thee to help me.[271]

Supernatural Veils

"But how is it that we now see through the Gate of Heaven into eternity?" "Pastor, when we look upon the account of Samson with our worldly eyes, we see a miserable picture. If you'll allow me, we see the Superman of the Old Testament that we call Samson misbehaving. And he behaved anything but Christ-like. Samson's account is painted upon a veil like a mask or a curtain with a pattern on it. On the surface of that mask we see a man that was given a great destiny, but he went astray, like Jonah, like David, like so many others. And Samson continually fell into sin because he lusted after worldly pleasures. It wasn't until the very end of Samson's life that he realized that his power was neither of himself nor for himself. His power was the Lord's. When Samson called upon the Lord his great power was restored." "So professor, what are we to make of Samson's account?"

"In many ways the account of Samson is our story. It's your story. God has given each one of us a Plan to do something special; a rescue plan for ourselves and those around us. But we've all fallen and lusted after the world. But if we'd call upon the Lord in our moment of helplessness, He'll be willing to reach down and rescue us. It's my story, it's Adam's story, and it's yours." "So the life of

---

271 Psalms 22:11-19.

Samson is used to hide the Plan of Salvation! I'm still trying to appreciate what you've revealed to me today. It's so overwhelming. So are you saying that the entirety of the Old Testament hid Jesus behind a veil like a person hides at a masquerade party behind a mask?" "Yes! You'll recall the writings of His servant Paul as we discussed earlier today."

> *But their minds were blinded: for until this day remaineth the same veil untaken away in the reading of the old testament; which [veil] is done away in Christ. But even unto this day, when Moses is read, the veil is upon their heart. Nevertheless when it shall turn to the Lord, the veil shall be taken away.*[272]

"Jesus and His Plan of Salvation are hidden behind the literal accounts of the Old Testament Guardians until He had secured the victory. Each Guardian's account adds to the dimensionality of Jesus like the beauty of a finely faceted jewel." "Professor the world today needs to be warned."

> *But as the days of Noe [were], so shall also the coming of the Son of man be. For as in the days that were before the flood they were eating and drinking, marrying and giving in marriage, until the day that Noe entered into the ark, And knew not until the flood came, and took them all away; so shall also the coming of the Son of man be.*[273]

Our incredible journey suddenly came to a screeching halt. We had arrived at the pastor's destination. And as he shook my hand the pastor said, "Professor, please don't forget to send me the book you're writing on Jonah. I'm very intrigued by what you've told me today and I can't wait to see how you unlock Jonah."

---

272 2 Corinthians 3:14-18.
273 Matthew 24:37-39.

EPILOGUE:
Guardians of the Code

That it might be fulfilled which was spoken by the prophet, saying, I will open my mouth in parables; I will utter things which have been kept secret from the foundation of the world.[274]

The Scriptures incorporate coded messages of the "*mysteries of the kingdom of God*"[275] "*kept secret from the foundation of the world*"[276] carefully concealed throughout Old Testament passages. The secrets are concealed that the enemies of the kingdom of heaven yet "*seeing they might not see, and hearing they might not understand.*"[277] The hidden secrets provide an ingenious plan to defeat the greatest threat ever to confront the Kingdom of God. Since the "*Fall of Mankind*" the world has been caught up in a supernatural war between Christ and Satan.[278] It would have been easy for our omnipotent God to defeat a created being like Satan. But God had to defeat Satan with love, since God's character is love.[279] According to the Scriptures the plan to rescue mankind from sin and death would have been lost[280] should this encrypted evidence have fallen into the hands of the enemy. The pinnacle of the secret plan was predicated upon the victory of the Cross:

...we speak the wisdom of God in a mystery, [even] the hidden [wisdom], which God ordained before the world unto our glory: Which none of the princes of this world

---

274 Matthew 13:35.
275 Luke 8:10.
276 Matthew 13:34, 35.
277 Luke 8:10.
278 Revelation 12:7, 17.
279 1 John 4:7-16.
280 1 Corinthians 2:7, 8.

knew: <u>for had they known [it], they would not have crucified the Lord of glory.</u>[281]

You see, we're told that if the plan were known by Satan and his forces, Christ would not have been crucified, and God's plan would have been foiled. Christ had to be crucified to rescue mankind. It was the ultimate proof of God's love and the ultimate proof that God cares. So the Scriptures had to be divinely encrypted[282] so that the forces of evil would be caught unaware. The unlocking of the coded messages of His death, burial, and resurrection had to be so compelling that there would be no doubt that God exists. The coded messages kept secret since the foundation of the world were the hidden evidence that would vindicate God. Even though Christ gained the victory over sin and death at the Cross, Satan continues to war with God's people for their souls.[283] Satan is doing everything he can to blind the minds of men so they can't see the Truth. Satan and his forces have blinded the minds of men by the veil of disbelief. And he is working hard to cause those that follow Christ to fall. But God has provided a Way of escape hidden within the pages of the Scriptures.

... their minds were blinded: for until this day remaineth the same veil untaken away in the reading of the old testament; which [veil] is done away in Christ.[284]

Yet, even unto this day, when the writings of Moses are read, the veil covers their hearts. All they need to do is turn to the Lord.

Nevertheless when it [the heart] shall turn to the Lord, the veil shall be taken away. Now the Lord is that Spirit: and where the Spirit of the Lord [is], there [is] liberty.[285]

---

281 1 Corinthians 2:7, 8.
282 Matthew 13:35
283 Revelation 12:17.
284 2 Corinthians 3:14.
285 2 Corinthians 3:16, 17.

The ancient Old Testament Scriptures hide a treasure map that provides the Way for us to gain freedom from sin and death. Once you find the golden keys and unlock the codes held by each Guardian, like Samson, Jonah, David, Joseph, Moses and many others and compile the composite treasure[286] map, it will provide you infallible proof that God exists. In one familiar account, the Scribes and Pharisees approached Jesus and mocked Him not believing that He was the Son of God. They were convinced that He was a fraud. So they mockingly asked Him to show them a miracle. They didn't expect a miracle and when they heard Jesus' response they were even more convinced that Jesus was a fraud. Instead of a physical sign or miracle, Jesus pointed to one of the golden keys hidden in the Old Testament scroll of the prophet Jonah. The golden key in the scroll of the prophet Jonah prophetically foretold that the Son of God must die, be buried, and be resurrected again over the short period of three days:

> *But he answered and said unto them, An evil and adulterous generation seeketh after a sign [miracle]; and there shall no sign be given to it, but the sign of the prophet Jonas: For as Jonas was three days and three nights in the whale's belly; so shall the Son of man be three days and three nights in the heart of the earth.*[287]

And referring to Himself, He said one "*greater than Jonas [is] here*." Jesus defiantly told them that He was the Son of man but they didn't comprehend the Scriptures because of their unbelief. Jesus gave the scribes and Pharisees one of the greatest miracles that He could have given them but they were too hard-hearted to understand. They had believed in a different paradigm. They believed that their Messiah would come from heaven and cast out the Romans and restore Israel to its former glory.

There is a miracle recorded in that little book. The miracle that Jesus pointed the scribes and Pharisees to was far more than the rescue of Jonah by a mysterious fish. He pointed them to the

---

286 Matthew 13:44.
287 Matthew 12:39, 40.

encryption of His death, burial, and resurrection. Jesus deliberately tipped His hand knowing that they were unbelievers and that they were spiritually blind. So why did He reveal the miracle? He made His reference to the miracle of Jonah so that many seeking the Truth like you and me would search the Scriptures after His death, burial, and resurrection and conclude that without a doubt, He is the Christ, the Son of the living God. Jesus words are as much for us today as they were for the scribes and Pharisees.

Guardian Keys

I [am] he that liveth, and was dead; and, behold, I am alive for evermore, Amen; and have the keys of hell and of death.[288] Had they taken Jesus seriously, they would have searched the scroll of Jonah to see if what Jesus was saying was true. But they thought they understood the scroll of Jonah and they couldn't see Christ in it. Today we're without excuse because we know that Jesus fulfilled the miraculous encryption that He had pointed out to the Scribes and Pharisees. But that's just the beginning; not the end. Numerous other Guardians like Samson and Jonah hold golden keys to unlock the hidden meaning behind passages that have unexplored depth of meaning. Each Guardian holds golden keys to unlock the coded messages of the history of the world and the future of mankind. Golden keys were hidden beforehand within the Old Testament accounts of **Guardians of the Code** like Samson, Moses, Solomon, David, Jonah, Abraham, Isaac, Daniel, Moses, Cyrus, and Joseph to name but a few. When their collection of golden keys are assembled a treasure map emerges that unlocks the evidence of the existence of God like an *"infallible proof."* The Scribes and Pharisees were incapable of unlocking the ancient scrolls because of disdain and disbelief but we are without excuse. Why are we able to unlock this supernatural code today? After His resurrection, Jesus told His followers:

---

288 Revelation 1:18.

... These [are] the words which I spake unto you, while I was yet with you, that all things must be fulfilled, which were written in the law of Moses, and [in] the prophets, and [in] the psalms, concerning me. <u>*Then opened he their understanding, that they might understand the scriptures,*</u> *And said unto them, Thus it is written, and thus it behoved Christ to suffer, and to rise from the dead the third day:*[289]

The prophecy of events that would occur in the life of Christ hundreds of years into the future was ingeniously veiled by symbols and parables within a supernatural multidimensional-cryptogram. The miracle of Jonah is a hidden message. Ask yourself how Jesus knew that His life would end in a manner like that spelled out ages before in the little book of Jonah. The symbolic connection between the *"death, burial, and resurrection"* of Jesus and Jonah is deliberate. **The connection was established by a supernatural Being long before the birth of Christ.** It is one of an extensive number of golden keys spelled out before the birth of Jesus that provides prophetic evidence that Jesus is the Christ. And even more amazingly, hundreds of prophecies hidden in the accounts of all the other Guardians had to be fulfilled as well. How could all the events in the lives of so many witnesses fit together? After years of investigation, I have determined that they are consistent and congruent; not contradictory and inconsistent. **That is the grand miracle of the Scriptures and the infallible evidence of GOD**. And with the golden keys we'll be able to unlock events that will lead to the last events of earth's history.

Hand Upon the Wheels

...then he went in, and stood beside the wheels. And [one] cherub stretched forth his hand from between the cherubims unto the fire that [was] between the cherubims, and took [thereof], and put [it] into the

289 Luke 24:44-45.

hands of [him that was] clothed with linen: who took [it], and went out.[290] ...having a live coal in his hand, [which] he had taken with the tongs from off the altar: And he laid [it] upon my mouth, and said, Lo, this hath touched thy lips; and thine iniquity is taken away, and thy sin purged. Also I heard the voice of the Lord, saying, Whom shall I send, and who will go for us? Then said I, Here [am] I; send me.[291]

Breaking the supernatural multidimensional-cryptogram of the Scriptures depends upon an understanding of the architecture of the Scriptures which are like wheels within wheels woven upon the Sanctuary fabric. As you read through the passages of the Old Testament you likely had the impression that you'd heard a similar thought elsewhere in the Bible like an echo. I'm sure you heard them calling from the shadows because many of the themes of the Scriptures are repeated to reinforce and enlarge upon a thought. On the other hand, portions of the Scriptures are filled with scenes that at first may seem impenetrable. But when one compares portions of the Scriptures with like passages elsewhere, the scenes become unlocked. The lives of each of the Old Testament characters are intertwined with one another and intertwined with the life of Christ and His Plan of Salvation.

The Scriptures are recorded on scrolls that are wrapped about axels and, as the scrolls are wound, the paper takes on a spiral-form just like the spiral of a galaxy. The handle end of each scroll appears as a wheel. And sets of scrolls have numerous wheels. The passages of the Scriptures are interconnected by words, literary images, phrases, metaphors and parables making what at first may seem as a disconnected collection of scrolls. But in reality they're woven together as a beautiful unified tapestry of the Plan of Salvation. In the big picture, the scrolls collectively record the history and future of mankind within the context of the war between God and Satan. In a way, you might say that the Scriptures are comprised of a set of scrolls bearing themes and

---

290 Ezekiel 10:6, 7.
291 Isaiah 6:6-8.

events that intersect, repeat and enlarge, and expand like the unfolding of a fern. From one perspective, you might view the intersection of the scrolls as wheels managed by the Hand of God as He controls the destiny of mankind. God is unfolding His Plan as surely as He is unfolding the plan He has for you. Will you accept the burning coal of salvation? Will you say Here I am; send me? Make your choice based on the evidence.

Events in history repeat themselves. Likewise, sequences of events in the Scriptures repeat themselves. That realization is exceedingly important and will become clearer as you unlock the mysterious Code held by other Guardians like Samson. Many scientists, academics, worldly writers, atheists, and agnostics struggle to come to terms with the hopelessness of a life that ends forever in death. Most of those that scoff at the Bible have never even read it. Or if they have, their reading has been so shallow that they've missed its hidden treasures.

Samson and a **_Great Cloud of Witnesses_** give us *infallible proofs*[292] and the *hope*[293] of everlasting life. They assure us that we didn't arrive on planet Earth by chance out of nothingness. Their testimonies prove that God exists and has set a plan in motion to save all those that believe in Him.

Scoffers of the Scriptures

Satan calls God a liar and impugns His Governing principles, His Commandments, His Laws, and His Character. Satan would have us believe that God doesn't exist, that the supernatural realm doesn't exist, that the world wasn't covered in a singular event that the Bible refers to as Noah's Flood. More importantly, Satan would have you believe that you and I are the consequence of millions upon millions of years of accidental chemical reactions that fumbled themselves from simple molecules to humans.

---

292 Acts 1:3.
293 Titus 2:13.

> *Knowing this first, that there shall come in the last days scoffers, walking after their own lusts, And saying, Where is the promise of his coming? for since the fathers fell asleep, all things continue as [they were] from the beginning of the creation. For this they willingly are ignorant of, that by the word of God the heavens were of old, and the earth standing out of the water and in the water: Whereby the world that then was, being overflowed with water, perished.*[294]

Who are these scoffers? They are the influential voices of the world that we depend upon for truth. They scoff at those who would believe in God based on their limited knowledge of the universe and planet Earth. Most of those that scoff at the Bible have never even read it. Because of their spiritual blindness they can't align the Scriptures with their perceptions of the cosmos and origins. To be sure, many scientists have stood for the existence of God including Newton and Einstein, but today they've fallen into the minority. Today's science has led many to believe that there's nothing but life and death. They give us no cause for hope or meaning to life.

The systematic implementation of our connections mysteriously tie not only Samson but a large cloud of Old Testament witnesses to the life of Christ, providing proof positive that they all share the same Supernatural Author. The ties are intricately woven within the text so that they would remain secret until the appointed time. And that time was marked by Christ's own words, *"It is finished: and he bowed his head, and gave up the ghost."*[295] And later at Christ's ascension, He was found worthy to open the Scriptures to mankind and reveal Himself on the road to Emmaus. When you consider the likelihood of 52 events occurring in the lives of two individuals born more than a thousand years apart the odds are staggering. But the odds are more staggering when you realize that the events in the account of Samson involve an Angel of the Lord, supernatural power, feats beyond comprehension like killing a lion

---

294 2 Peter 3:3-6.
295 John 19:30.

Pattern of Samson's Account Points to Christ

Account of Samson	Divine Pair Miracle Births		Account of Jesus
Angel announces birth to mother	2	2	Angel announces birth to Mary
Born a Nazarite	3	3	Nazarene: Lives in Nazareth
Angel announces birth to Father	5	5	Angel announces birth to Joseph
"Like the Sun"	7	7	"Sun of Righteousness"
Driven by spirit	8	8	Driven by spirit into wilderness
Defeats Lion	12	12	Defeats Devil as a roaring Lion
Wedding Garments	16	16	Wedding Garments
Sends them 2 by 2	21	21	Sends apostles 2 by 2
Set fields on fire	23	23	Apostles set world on fire
Jawboning	26	26	Preaching
Great Slaughter	27	27	Converts hearts among 5000
Kills them Hip and Thigh	29	29	Converts hearts among 4000
Ends Speaking	30	30	Ends Speaking
Plot to Kill Samson	31	31	Plot to Kill Jesus
Gates cannot prevail	32	32	Gates of hell cannot prevail
Betrayed by the woman: Delilah	35	35	Betrayed by His own
Lords of Philistines	36	36	Lords of Pharisees
Sold for silver	37	37	Sold for silver
Power in the 7 Locks	40	40	Power in the 7 Horns
Blinded	41	41	Blindfolded
Bound	42	42	Bound
Imprisoned	43	43	Imprisoned
Dagon	46	46	Satan
Make sport of him	47	47	Make sport of Him
Outstretched Arms	48	48	Outstretched Arms
Destroys House of false god	49	49	Destroys House of false god
Kills more in death than life	50	50	Converts more in death than life
Judged Israel 20 Years	52	52	Judges Israel

bare handed, or capturing 300 foxes and tying their tails together to a firebrand, or killing a thousand men with a jawbone of an ass on two occasions, or bringing down a temple with his bare hands. The use of scientific methods proves that there's a supernatural world that science hasn't accounted for and that proof changes everything. The amazing cryptogram gives us all the evidence we need without taking a leap of faith. We don't have to believe that nothing comes from nothing. Based on the hidden code behind the account of Samson we know that God exists. How else can you explain how the writers of the Old Testament documented detailed information about Jesus more than a thousand years in advance? Events connecting the Old and New Testaments are intentionally embedded and choreographed through symbolic encryption so that the life records of Jesus Christ and Samson, along with many other Old Testament characters, would be positively linked as if by supernatural DNA.

Statistics

What are the odds of these 52 events being so clearly connected? If you were to take two decks of cards and ask two individuals to select a card and place it down on the table and record it and then have each individual replace the card back in the deck, shuffle, and repeat the draw 52 times between them, what is the likelihood that the cards will be in order from one to 52? This can be expressed as 52 factorial or 8×10^{67}. The number will, in my estimation, exceed finding a single atom out of all of the atoms in the Planet Earth! Suffice it to say it is an almost incomprehensibly big number. And when you consider that 7 Guardians have 52 or more events that parallel events in the life of Christ, it is like finding a single atom among all the atoms of the universe. We can only conclude that the code that connects the lives of Samson and Jesus was deliberately hidden. Just as the Bible tells us, the links were made secret until after the work of Jesus was completed at the Cross more than a thousand years after His every step was encrypted.

Every step that Jesus took while he walked the Earth, from His birth to His resurrection and ascension was known more than a thousand years in advance in great detail. In speaking to the Jews, Jesus said ***Search the scriptures; for in them ye think ye have eternal life: and they are they which testify of me***.[296] By this Jesus meant that the Jews thought their path to heaven was through their traditions. Jesus proved that the traditions in the Scriptures were all about Him through the testimonies of His Guardians who testify that He is the only Way to eternal life.

At the beginning of my journey, I assumed that the evidence would demonstrate that the Scriptures were authored by men; not God. How could an evolutionist justify the Scriptural accounts of a world-wide flood or Creation? The two are appear to be at odds. I was initially convinced that the Scriptures would fail because of inconsistent and incongruent arguments by comparing literal accounts. That is, I fully expected to find that the logic in the New Testament would be contradicted by the literal patterns of the Old Testament. Instead, the encoded patterns prove that **God Exists as the Scriptures claim**.

Supernatural Universe?

Do beings from an invisible Universe really interfere with your life and destiny? Or does mankind just dream this up as an excuse to cover-up our guilt for the sins we commit? The account of Samson in the Book of Judges reads more like Greek mythology than a factual account of events. Either the account of Samson is factual due to Supernatural intervention or it is fable or legend. After all, how could a single man kill more than a thousand men, on more than one occasion, with the jawbone of an ass?

Is there any evidence of a supernatural universe? Supernatural events described in the Bible and in the accounts of writers like Roger Morneau[297] can't be explained by the natural laws of the physical world. According to their accounts, objects can be tossed by unseen hands, people can be possessed, and our lives can be

---

296 John 5:39.
297 A Trip into the Supernatural. Roger J. Morneau. Review and Herald Publishing, Hagerstown, MD. 1982.

shattered by invisible beings. To a scientific observer such events would appear to defy the laws of physics.

The Bible claims that angels can enter into a human body as a host. The insidious notion that unseen beings can enter into a human host, like the demoniac,[298] hasn't been explained by modern science or medicine. The Scriptures record other instances where invisible beings supposedly enter the bodies of their unsuspecting victims and control their destiny. It's even said that Satan entered into the apostle Peter[299] in a devilish attempt to trick Christ and cause Him to fall. The Scriptures claim that it was Satan that entered into Judas Iscariot[300] and bartered with the Jewish fathers to crucify Jesus using the willing yet unsuspecting mind of Judas. The Scriptures make it clear that your body can be entered by a fallen angel or a "demon" that can take over your very thoughts and worse yet, direct your actions! Could there be any truth to the saying *"the devil made me do it?"* We're told that demons shackle and imprison you by temptation, just as Satan tried to tempt Christ. Scientists shrug this all off as fantasy. In 1956, the well-known film, the *Invasion of the Body Snatchers,* was released.[301] Could it actually have been unsuspectingly based upon fact rather than fiction? According to Morneau,[302] Satan, the fallen angel once known as Lucifer in heaven, is very real. Morneau tells of how he fell into a satanic cult in Montreal and lived to tell about it. He gives compelling details about how famous public figures are propped up and destroyed by Satan's legions. And he tells of how unseen supernatural forces can toss physical objects, cause fires, and destroy lives. He even gives accounts of the voices of demons

---

298 Mark 5:7-9 …What have I to do with thee, Jesus, [thou] Son of the most high God? I adjure thee by God, that thou torment me not. For he said unto him, Come out of the man, [thou] unclean spirit. And he asked him, What [is] thy name? And he answered, saying, My name [is] Legion: for we are many.
299 Mark 8:33 But when he had turned about and looked on his disciples, he rebuked Peter, saying, Get thee behind me, Satan…
300 Luke 22:3 Then entered Satan into Judas surnamed Iscariot, being of the number of the twelve.
301 Invasion of the Body Snatchers. Jack Finney. Dell Publishing. 1956.
302Morneau, Roger, A Trip into the Supernatural, Review and Herald. 1982, 1993.

speaking through their human hosts. Some say that Satan was behind the theories of Darwin! Could this be true? Did Satan enter into Darwin and so control his mind that Satan through Darwin espoused the theory of evolution to confound scientists and our science? Before Darwin, many like Sir Isaac Newton were believers. Could Satan have deceived the bastions of Science? After all, the vast majority of scientists today are aligned with Darwin. Some churches now even accept evolution! Evolution seems to contradict the Bible. Doesn't it?

Today, like in no previous era in world history, we're being bombarded by television, hand-held computers, smart phones, wrist phones, and the radio which, according to the Scriptures, are being used by these unseen forces. Are these media being used by fallen angels to program our thinking? Paul writes about the *"prince of the power of the air, the spirit that now worketh in the children of disobedience."* Radio waves and other media are transmitted through the air. Are these the vehicles that the Scriptures warn us about? The Apostle Paul warns us that *"we wrestle not against flesh and blood, but against principalities, against powers, against the rulers of the darkness of this world, against spiritual wickedness in high [places]."* Could any of this be true? Does science have a responsibility to explore the possibility that the Bible is truth? Since the days of Darwin, the scientific community has strangely turned its back on the Bible. Why have scientists strangely walked away from the study of the Scriptures and the supernatural?

Wherefore seeing we also are compassed about with so great a cloud of witnesses, let us lay aside every weight, and the sin which doth so easily beset [us], and let us run with patience the race that is set before us, Looking unto Jesus the author and finisher of [our] faith; who for the joy that was set before him endured the cross, despising the shame, and is set down at the right hand of the throne of God. [Hebrews 12:1, 2.]

APPENDIX:
Spiritual Archaeology

Which things also we speak, not in the words which man's wisdom teacheth, but which the Holy Ghost teacheth; comparing spiritual things with spiritual. But the natural man receiveth not the things of the Spirit of God: for they are foolishness unto him: neither can he know [them], because they are spiritually discerned.[303]

Gospel Templates

After numerous years of study, I'm convinced that the most important keys to unlocking much of the Old Testament are the four Gospel accounts. The combined Gospels serve as a template of the event time sequence based on the recorded sequence in the earthly walk of Christ. I use the four Gospels as my key by superimposing the timeline of events that occur in the Gospel accounts on Old Testament accounts like Samson. My approach allows me to identify obvious parallel points. I use this approach just as an archaeologist uses a map or key to locate treasure. The hidden accounts in the Old Testament records are in parallel alignment with the Gospels. I've learned through experience that this method is essential to assuring reproducible results.

Event Sequence Analysis

With the four Gospels as a back-drop, I use modern applications of event sequence analysis to evaluate the Old Testament texts. It is much like stratigraphic correlation applied by earth scientists for mineral and oil deposits, and it is used by geneticists to correlate

---

303 1 Corinthians 2:13, 14.

gene sequences. Methods of event sequence analysis are rapidly being transformed by automated methods. For example, the University of Maryland has developed software, referred to as EventFlow: A Visual Analysis of Temporal Events.[304] The software has been used throughout the medical, social, and physical sciences.

> Eventflow has been used for medical research, log analysis, cybersecurity, sports analytics, learning analytics, incident management, workflow analysis, pharmacovigilance, epidemiology etc. The analysis of healthcare data has been our main focus in term of number of partners.

> Medical researchers and hospitals have applied EventFlow to analyze treatment patterns and outcomes in Electronic Health Records or claims reports, while network security analysts have studied cyberattack patterns and sports analysts have found novel approaches to studying games, overall team performance, and seasonal patterns. Education researchers and universities have used EventFlow to look at class enrollment sequences and student records. Applications for web log, sensor data, business processes, and financial transactions are also emerging markets.

Event sequence analysis methods are:

> …methods seeking patterns that recur across a number of sequences. They are applied to data on social sequences (occupational careers or life courses, for example) as well as to historical sequences (of policy adoption, for example) and cultural sequences (different versions of a particular story, for example). The most common techniques for sequence analysis are optimal matching techniques, so-called because they operate by finding distances between pairs of sequences on the basis of an 'optimal match' of the two sequences—a minimal series of operations that transform one sequence into the other. In computer science,

---

304 http://hcil.umd.edu/eventflow/

the optimal matching problem is usually called the string alignment problem. In social sequence analysis, the matrix of pairwise distances between sequences is used in any standard two-way analysis scheme like scaling or cluster analysis to produce categorizations or dimensionalizations of a sequence space.[305]

Literary Light is Illumination

The Scriptures are laid upon a wave form that serves as a fabric throughout the entire Bible. In my opinion, the waves can be considered as a form of literary light.

When you look at the waves you realize that they provide evolving messages that illuminate hidden themes. Each wave builds on a previous wave. The waves transform thought and meaning from a simple concept to a deeper and more complete concept. The fabric can contain words that are expressed as synonyms, antonyms, or even complex thoughts on each side of the waves, or they can contrast meanings to expand the thought. Some call these chiastic structures but they are far more than simple localized poetic patterns. The fabric is the key to illumination.

You might say that the overall fabric of the Scriptures are spiral-form like the shape of spiral galaxies. This spiral-form weave extends from one end of the Scriptures to the other. How could such a pattern have been orchestrated for thousands of years?

Literary Algebra

The third key is what I refer to as Literary Algebra. By that I mean that the multi-dimensional, metaphor, or riddle painted by the author on the physical level often has another deeper meaning on the spiritual level. Each element in the equation has symbolic meaning. God's writings are designed to be engaging and thought-

305 International Encyclopedia of the Social and Behavioral Sciences, 2001. Pages 4966–4969. Elsevier.

provoking. Riddles, parables, and metaphors are woven into the fabric to produce a mental image. The writings of God's Plan of Salvation is presented, by design, in a way that we can long remember.

It's a form of what Intelligence Agency code workers today refer to as steganography.[306] These agencies and others have been using physical images to conceal codes for a very long time. Today they can hide massive detailed encrypted instructions in a picture or a video. You could be watching a seemingly harmless TV show but...behind it an intelligence agency or hacker could encode it with subliminal messages, even video! They could even be gathering information about you and the members of your household.

By contrast the Bible uses Word pictures in contrast to a physical picture. The meaning of the algebraic word picture is unlocked by comparing it to its place in the Scriptures and next by comparing the scenes of the word picture with similar words, phrases, or thoughts found elsewhere at parallel points in the timeline of the four Gospels. The correlation is often through the symbolic imagery that connects the physical world to the supernatural world.

The Scriptures are filled with symbolic words, phrases, and literary imagery...like the parables and riddles that Christ used as a tool for teaching. The approach is kind of like ancient Egyptian hieroglyphics on steroids. Many of the scenes in the account of Samson are like a picture or parable if you like. The literary picture has at least dual meanings. And when you translate the dual meaning and paste it on a time line, you realize that the events in the life of Samson are in the same order as they appear in the life of Christ.

---

306 Steganography—The New Intelligence Threat. EWS 2004. Subject Area Intelligence. Murphy, S.D.

Multiple Meanings of Words

A single word can have multiple meanings. Often times that's the key to unlocking portions of the Scriptures. Every word, every phrase, every jot and tittle[307] needs to be studied. Check out Strong's Concordance.[308] My wife taught me to use Strong's Concordance reveal the original meaning of words in the Hebrew and Greek. And analyzing each word and phrase in the original context proves to be a powerful means of unlocking the text.

Other Books by the Author

Guardians: Keepers of God's Secret Code: provides an example of the Harmony of Types through 7 Old Testament characters and the Wilderness Sanctuary as figures of Christ's life.

Apocalypse Now: The Rocks Cry Out: provides a technical basis for global flooding and the catastrophic origin of the primary features of Earth that challenges evolution.

To Save the Lost

This book is dedicated to saving the lost. Profits will be used to support evangelism campaigns, presentations at Vacation Bible Schools, and special presentations upon request. The profits will also be used to build churches, provide support to Christian schools, and ***Defend the poor and fatherless: [to] do justice to the afflicted and needy. Deliver the poor and needy: [and] rid [them] out of the hand of the wicked***.[309]

---

307 Matthew 5:18.
308 Strong, James (1890), The Exhaustive Concordance of the Bible, Cincinnati: Jennings & Graham.
309 Psalm 82:3, 4.

ABOUT THE AUTHOR

Dr. Don Alexander served as lead geochemist in US NRC's Office of Nuclear Materials Safeguards and Security (NMSS) where he helped develop regulations for the disposition of High Level Waste. He later worked for DOE's Office of Civilian Radioactive Waste Management (OCRWM), serving as a liaison to the Nuclear Energy Agency in Paris. At OCRWM, he managed the development of Site Characterization Plans for the evaluation of a U.S. National Repository. With DOE's Office of Energy Waste Management (EM), he led International Technology Program missions to the Former Soviet Union (FSU), Japan, France, England, Italy, Germany, Hungary, and throughout Europe. He led a mission to the FSU and established the first exchange of scientists working on nuclear waste programs between the United States Department of Energy's National Laboratories and the Former Soviet Union. In that capacity, he negotiated for the transfer of Russian data on the effects of radiation on workers and civilians in the Urals. Don taught for a number of years as a Clinical Professor in the Department of Environmental Health Sciences, Tulane University School of Public Health and Tropical Medicine and served as PhD Co-Chair for three dissertations.

Don holds a Doctorate of Philosophy in Geology, specializing in Geochemistry, from the University of Michigan

www.ingramcontent.com/pod-product-compliance
Lightning Source LLC
Chambersburg PA
CBHW031250090426
42742CB00007B/387